MY BOSS IS A BASTARD

OVERCOMING THE BOSS FROM HELL

Richard Maun

Disclaimer

Please note: Any resemblance to any person or business contained within this book is purely coincidental. If you think you know of someone in any of the examples, you are mistaken. I was writing about someone else.

Copyright © 2006 Richard Maun
Artwork supplied by Rebecca Maun, www.richardmaun.com

First published in 2006
This edition published in 2012 by Marshall Cavendish Business
An imprint of Marshall Cavendish International
1 New Industrial Road, Singapore 536196
genrefsales@sg.marshallcavendish.com
www.marshallcavendish.com/genref

Other Marshall Cavendish offices: Marshall Cavendish Corporation. 99 White Plains Road, Tarrytown NY 10591-9001, USA • Marshall Cavendish International (Thailand) Co Ltd. 253 Asoke, 12th Flr, Sukhumvit 21 Road, Klongtoey Nua, Wattana, Bangkok 10110, Thailand • Marshall Cavendish (Malaysia) Sdn Bhd. Times Subang, Lot 46, Subang Hi-Tech Industrial Park, Batu Tiga, 40000 Shah Alam, Selangor Darul Ehsan, Malaysia

Marshall Cavendish is a trademark of Times Publishing Limited

The right of Richard Maun to be identified as the author of this work has been asserted by him in accordance with the Copyright, Designs and Patents Act 1988.

A CIP record for this book is available from the British Library

ISBN 978-981-4382-35-9

Printed and bound in the United Kingdom by TJ International

For FMM Intake 52,
who helped me to wake up
and for Beck, who is just great.

Other Marshall Cavendish career books
by Richard Maun

Bouncing Back
How to get going again after a career setback

How to Keep Your Job
Brilliant ways to increase performance, stay employed
and keep the money rolling in

Job Hunting 3.0
Secrets and skills to sell yourself effectively
in the modern age

Leave The B@$T@*DS Behind
An insider's guide to working for yourself

Books are available in hard copy and electronic formats

Contents

Preface

This book has been written to help people reflect on their own stressful situations and to help them think about what they can do to move forwards. Whether you have lost your job, or are stuck in a miserable position with a boss who treats you like the living dead, this book is here to help.

We spend our working lives under the harsh glare of a corporate sun that defies the laws of space and time and often makes up its own rules, so it's crucial to keep our water bottles of learning topped up and to take regular swigs to prevent dehydration. However, because some management books are as appetizing as stale bread, this one has been written to make your taste buds sit up and samba. It's a delicious savoury morsel, designed to make your tongue lick your lips and make your mouth beg for seconds.

The tips, comments, ideas and questions contained within *My Boss is a Bastard* have been based on real experiences. They are designed to encourage people to think about where they are, where they would like to be and what practical steps they can take to remedy their situation.

If you read *My Boss is a Bastard* and smile, that's great. If you read it and remember one thing, that's fantastic. However, if you read it and take one genuine step to increase your inner health then treat yourself to a lap of honour around your local supermarket, because you win the gold medal. Well done.

However, as most people have had to cope with a bum job or a boss with questionable parentage, we may as well have some fun along the way. Therefore, this book is full of naughty words and cheeky illustrations of our spiky world of work. You have been warned.

Before we start on the journey towards increasing our inner happiness it's worth noting that I am in a happy place. A life spent in work is always going to be a mixture of good times and good bosses and stressful times with stressed bosses. I've had an interesting mixture of both and all of them have helped me to go forwards in some way. So, thanks go to them for their support and we all know that no one is really a bastard. That is just a handy nail to hang our hat on when our emotions are raging like a river in flood.

However, tough decisions do have to be made sometimes and collateral damage is unavoidable, so the purpose of this book is to focus people on what they can do for themselves. Spare a thought for the manager who has to let you go. He (or she) has probably sweated their way through breakfast and journeyed to work with ice in their stomach, wishing the day away before it has even started.

When people have a tough job to do they are under pressure and the stress can make them act out of awareness. They can forget the pleasantries that make us human and go about their task in a methodical and dispassionate manner. There is a job to do and the doing of it does not make them someone to pillory in later life. They would tend to do it differently if they had another chance, so don't be too judgemental. All managers, of all types, have to earn a living and everyone deserves a chance to get it wrong from time to time.

As you read this book, use it as an opportunity to get in touch with your anger. Instead of using it to castigate someone who was doing the best job they could at the time, use it to focus your boiling energy on yourself. Everyone is entitled to a life and you may not like what other people say, or what they do, but that is no reason to let it deprive you of the chance of doing something more rewarding. Invest your energy in you.

Anger is a useful emotion and it's okay to feel angry. It's also important to find safe ways of expressing our anger. A great way is for people to use it to generate a head of steam, to create the momentum required to invest time and energy in their own future. Please don't simply rage at those who had a job to do, as that would be to miss the point. Instead read this book and think of yourself and where you want to be.

Finally, before we rush off into the World of Bastard there are a few people who need to be thanked. Nothing is ever produced in splendid isolation and without the help and support of the generous few this book would be just an idea, floating round the ether.

First up, take a bow Steve Tracey for your solid support and useful insights. Next up is Alan Robertson, who gets a big cheer for laughing out loud and being generous with his time. Frances Donnelly gets a well-earned round of applause for her advice and thoughtfulness, as does Martin Liu for his encouragement. Thank you to all my family and friends who took the time to read the manuscript (you know who you are) and finally a large bouquet of fresh flowers goes to my wife Beck, who supported me through all the dark days and out into the light again and who is always loving, tolerant and supportive.

Read, enjoy, think and make progress: it's not about them – it's about you.

Richard Maun
Norfolk, England

Richard can be contacted via:
Modern Careers Blog: www.richardmaun.com
Facebook Page: Richard Maun – Modern Careers
LinkedIn: Richard Maun
Twitter: @RichardMaun
Skype: richardmaun
Business: www.primarypeople.co.uk

Come in out of the Rain
Getting started

Please give me your attention for a moment. There is something we need to get clear before reading on. This book contains strong language, scenes of a violent nature and some sexy bits. Later there is a reference to a heaving bosom and, to ensure an even balance between the sexes, a large and excited bulge in the trouser department.

What? Why? Well, because life is like that. So, if these things are likely to offend your delicate sensibilities then pop this book back on the shelf and walk on by. You are not going to like it.

And because this book contains stories and anecdotes collected from many sources, you need to know that they have all been dressed up in false noses and scruffy wigs. The job of the book is not to identify the guilty, the stupid or the just plain incompetent. Any resemblance to someone you think you know, or a business which sounds familiar is purely coincidental.

One more thing, whilst we are in the disclaiming zone.

The author assumes that you are of sound mind and are able to make your own decisions, because you shall remain responsible for all of your actions or inactions that you take as a result of reading this book. If you don't like the sound of these two disclaimers then there's another reason to stick the book back on the shelf and let someone else buy it.

You would like to read on? You understand that you are your own person? Your expensive legal eagle is back in his eyrie? Okay then, let's do it and remember:

Read, enjoy, think and make progress: it's not about them – it's about you.

Have you ever come home from work, shut the door behind you and screamed out:

"I hate my job!" Or,

"I'm so stressed!" Or,

"My boss is a COMPLETE BASTARD!"

Or variations on the above that describe in minute detail just what your boss can do with his executive palmtop that will make it very awkward for the computer department to install new software without the aid of rubber gloves, lubricating jelly and a tyre lever. You have?

Then you are not alone. This book is for people who are fed up with a dull job, or with being taken advantage of at work. Fed up with working for a boss who has their best interests firmly placed at the bottom of his (or her) to-do list, after "order new flipchart" and "empty the waste basket".

And fed up with creaking management books that contain 10,000 top tips to stay in tip-top condition. Some have merit, others less so, but in a crisis the vast majority are about as useful as a hot air balloon in an aerial dogfight. Rat-tat-tat-tat-tat and down you go, sinking towards the enemy lines with only a silk scarf and a pair of goggles for company. And no parachute, because you thought it was too nerdy to carry one.

During an ass-kicking session, no one is going to hold up their hand and say:

"Excuse me old chap, I'm feeling a touch stressed and need to come up with some positive actions to counteract your vicious onslaught. Do you mind if I pop out to consult the library?"

This book is here to help us through these situations and to smooth the brow of the worried person.

In times of crisis we do not have six months to speed read the syllabus of a business course, or have access to a top-flight psychologist, who can sit in his comfy leather swivel chair, stroke his carefully manicured goatee beard and say: "Now zen my leetle koala bear, take me back to your childhood and together ve can unravel ze enigma zat is your current predicament."

No. Not in a million years. However, we probably have a network of worried family and friends who can mop our beading foreheads and give us a few handy hints. We also have our single greatest asset. Ourselves.

You are smart. We are all smart. We choose to do different things with our intellect. Some "clever" people let theirs rot, whilst other "stupid" people seem to climb effortlessly to greatness. Your first smart move is to do something for yourself, namely, to read on.

This book is here to give people some basic kit to survive when everything is shooting up in flames. Basic kit, mind you. Nobody ever ran out of a burning building, carrying their treasured grand piano. And basic is plenty in a world that wants the decision and wants it NOW.

In a crisis we experience a sort of inner weightlessness, when our stomach drops through our butt-hole and our brain does a gold medal winning series of back-flips, with half pike and twist. When this happens bulky equipment is not going to be of much use to us.

Think of this book as the equivalent of a good set of instructions tucked into a box of flat-pack furniture. At some point during the assembly of your deluxe mahogany shower cubicle you are going to get really cross with the effing effort of screwing Panel F to Upright G and insist that some sod in the factory has left out the special joining tool. This, of course, is the tool which you carelessly slung out with the packaging. In terms of a flat pack stress-out, simple guidelines are needed. Not simple because you are stupid. No, simple because your emotions are running high and your brain is likely to struggle with complex instructions written in techno-babble.

The next time you're out for a Saturday afternoon stroll, slip into your local camping shop and ask for a survival kit. Serious money suggests you'll only be able to buy a basic one, so don't bother asking the spotty counter-jockey for a complex kit in a gold posing pouch. So, in the spirit of practicality, this book will concentrate on simple and straightforward principles and here is the key one: travel light.

Travelling light means you can run fast. Go for a small amount of portable learning instead of a large ball and chain that will slow you down and spoil the cut of your designer business uniform.

It's a safe bet that none of us can remember what we had for dinner a week last Thursday.

Pasta?

Pork chops?

Honey roast ham?

It might as well have been Peacock pie with a Humming bird sauce for all the difference it makes. It's hardly surprising that when we're under real pressure our carefully learned models evaporate between our sizzling ears, leaving behind only the imprint of some dusty old knowledge.

Maslow may have had a hierarchy of needs, but is this going to stop you from getting shafted by some sweating Suit with a corporate leer? No, of course it's not. When the chips go down and the balloon goes up there is no time for in-depth research, or prolonged packing. You have to fight, jump, leap, swim or run.

You have no choice.

And when you have no choice and have to run for it, it helps to have some basic kit, a rough plan and a handful of options. To be of real value they need to be easily remembered, so here's a useful nugget to keep in your jacket pocket, or in a secret compartment in one of your shoes: Your PERSONAL SURVIVAL KIT. Where is yours? Do you even have one?

Well you do now.

Your Personal Survival Kit is the one item that will help you to stay in control of yourself and support you when navigating through the stinging hailstorm of a tough time. You don't need to have a leather-bound ermine-trimmed 64-meg Personal Survival Kit either, because a scruffy, dog-eared one will do just fine. When a poor unfortunate pilot is shot down and captured, his treatment is not based on the quality of the stuff he carries.

"Ah, look here Ivan, this pilot has a monogrammed survival kit. You sir can check into the local five star hotel. Enjoy your stay for the rest of the war and help yourself to the mini bar. No Ivan, the co-pilot has a cheap plastic kit with a crack in the lid. For you my friend it's off to the back of the bike sheds for some interrogation by big Sven."

So in the back of this book there is a Personal Survival Kit (PSK) for you to complete. In a time of crisis it may be your best friend. It may even be your only friend. It will become one of your key sources of handy information and guiding principles. But please don't turn to it and scribble in stuff now, because you need to think carefully about what to write.

To help the process of compilation there are regular prompts throughout the book. When you reach one it will invite you to complete a particular section of your PSK, so that when you reach the end of the book you will have completed the whole kit. Simple. We like simple.

The word Survival is intentional. This is because you have to survive first in order to make your escape. If your current situation is rotten then you may need to sneak your way to freedom, slipping with a smile past the noses of the guards, who are trained to shout:

"Stop! You can't do that!"

Yes you can.

You can do what you like, if you really want to.

Your Personal Survival Kit should be available to support you in an emergency situation and it's important to play fair and complete all the sections. Otherwise you could find yourself with some crucial bits missing at the wrong time.

This would be the survival equivalent of forgetting your compass, or your box of matches. You could try and start a fire by rubbing two boy scouts together, but getting a spark out of them will take until well past teatime and the authorities generally frown on this technique. When you're stuck in the wilderness, no amount of imagination is going to turn a broken twig into a magnetic needle, or into a fishhook, so please remember that a complete kit is essential.

Think of an emergency situation at work as if you had an exam suddenly sprung on you. Remember the last exam you sat and recall the rising panic and racing pulse that you experienced? If you don't go to work and are living in a tropical rain forest, remember the time you sweated when shooting your first arrow through a rare bird of paradise. Watch out, if you were raised in a forest and have never heard of management theory, because a brace of missionary consultants will be flying in to convert you any moment now.

Make use of them.

A pot roast for two is the most popular choice. They'll probably both fit into a decent sized pot.

However, whether you live in the jungle, in the city, or in some sleepy garden suburb, you should be aware of an English chap by the name of Thomas Hobbes (1588–1679). By day he was an ace political thinker and by night he was the homebrew king of Malmesbury. A fact which seems to have slipped out of the history books. Unhindered by the frailties of the modern PC, Tom thought and wrote and thought and wrote, buoyed up by the occasional yard of ale and foot of snuff. Despite never having heard the words "fat cat salaries" he would have well understood the current nature of our working world when he wrote in his 1651 masterpiece *Leviathan*:

"The goals we have are the satisfaction of our desires … of which the most fundamental are the desires to stay alive and avoid pain."

That's very true Tom, but what do you think about the life of man?

"The life of man is solitary, poor, nasty, brutish and short."

Thank you.

Good old Thomas Hobbes. Dead, but still useful. "Nasty, brutish and short" is a great summary of our world of work and can often be applied to fast food hotdogs.

Pull on a glittery shirt and waltz down to your local night club. Once inside, throw a stick and watch it bounce off someone who would cheerily agree that working for Super-Duper-Mega Inc was indeed nasty, brutish and short. They will have been stressed by Nasty, tripped up by Brutish and stabbed in the back by Short. Ouch.

Some people moan that life is dull. Dull? Really? Life is never dull. We live a life that is full of pace and passion and change. We live in a world that is being torn apart and stitched back together on a daily basis. People change their clothes, their hair colour and even the number of wrinkles on their face. Nothing can be taken for granted and nothing is above our meddling.

Famously though, leopards do not change their spots and look how badly they're doing!

Talking of change, the years 1831 to 1836 were vintage ones, when a ship called the HMS Beagle sailed round the world. Nothing remarkable in that you may think, although it was a very long way to go without bumping into anything sharp, armed or terminal. However, this sturdy vessel carried an inquisitive fellow by the name of Charles Robert Darwin. A capital chap, who was just itching to get cracking with new research and new learning.

Eventually after many months of ship biscuits, weevils and avoiding the unwanted attentions of lonely sailors he fetched up on the Galapagos Islands. Just short of the bit on the map marked "here be dragons". On the warm sands of his new home he passed the time trimming his beard, chasing finches and using the giant tortoises as slow moving coffee tables. Eventually, with his beard in a capital condition, he dug out his writing kit and knuckled down to some seriously hard work.

Days, weeks and tortoises all passed by and eventually his discount jotters were bursting with interesting observations and blots of inky inspiration. Finally, he had collected enough material to write a book and so he retreated back to his study in England, with sand in his socks and a suspiciously slow moving toast rack for company.

His weighty masterpiece called *On the Origin of Species by means of Natural Selection* was published in 1859 and at a stroke it introduced our forefathers and our foremothers to the word. And the word was EVOLUTION.

The world as viewed through our corporate binoculars evolves at a frightening speed and only those who evolve with it will survive and prosper. Those who do not wish to evolve are still worthy of our respect, but ultimately are not racehorses worth betting on. Someone, who should have known better, once commented:

"Evolution is all very well, but it's in the past. Nothing for *me* to worry about."

Of course, this person lived on their own personal desert island, where luxury hampers were airlifted in each week and all they did from dawn to dusk was sunbathe, snorkel and make sweet love to the sound of the whispering ocean.

If only life was that simple.

Here's a quick exercise to prove the point. What can you see that did not exist when you were a child? Put this book down and look around you.

Take a long look.

It's a long list, far longer than you might realize. Dust off the bookshelves in your mind and flick through what you know about medicine, electronics, communications, textiles and food.

There are many items in everyday use that we did not have as children and in some cases there are things that didn't even exist as recently as last year. To really make the point take a walk round your house and put a sticky label on everything you didn't have as a child. You will use up a frightening number of labels.

By the time you have read this book someone somewhere will have invented a radical new gizmo that you didn't know you needed. However you'll still shell out hard earned cash for one next Christmas, because it is just *so* indispensable. Of course, not all new inventions and gadgets are useful, but we buy them all the same. We don't mind really, we just want them because they are new and new means good and good means progress.

This book is about making progress. Making progress with your asshole of a boss and making progress with yourself. So, go on, treat yourself to a large slice of progress, with extra mozzarella and garlic bread.

Come in out of the rain. It's cold and wet outside. It's snug and warm inside. And full of strong language and spiky stories.

Why?

Because life is like that.

Roll up, Roll up
Who are we talking about?

Let's be clear about the precise nature of whom we are talking about. When we say "boss", we are talking about everyone who has control over our working lives. There is no rule that says being a prize Turd-on-a-Stick is solely confined to the male bosses out there. So roll up, roll up, ladies and gentlemen and please listen carefully. When we say "bastard", we of course mean bitch and their plurals bastards and bitches. We could attempt a collective noun, but the fun is in choosing your own. Try these for size to give your imagination a shove:

A leap of leopards.

A murder of crows.

A skulk of foxes.

A boardroom of self-abusers.

The first three are proper examples, whereas the fourth is probably not a literal truth, but the sort of thing that people say with feeling when their company has just announced record losses, or allowed the directors to help themselves to a generous pay rise, whilst telling the workforce that restraint is needed. Or when the corporate lights have been switched off and you have a mortgage payment to meet.

Bosses come in all shapes and sizes. And sexes. And smells. And nationalities. They can be called team leaders, supervisors, charge hands, managers, directors, chairmen or (potentially the most odious) live-in consultants.

Broadly speaking there are two kinds of consultant:

Type A, who turn up at work for a couple of days, provide you with some useful insights and then piss off from whence they came. These people are generally useful and mostly harmless. Then there are their shadowy cousins from the distant marshes:

Type B, who start off by assuring the management that they are only going to be on site for a short period of time, but then stay forever. Like poison ivy wrapping itself around a tree, they live on without killing their host, but without really providing any useful function. Be warned, because although these people do not fit neatly into the organization chart they have immense influence and they may well be after a job. Your job. So watch out.

We'll use the term "boss" to define anyone in a position of authority over you and the word "bastard" because it's pithy and because that's how people talk. If you prefer your own version of bastard, please feel free to deface your copy of this book, assuming of course that you are not still in the bookshop. If you are, at least have the decency to pay for the thing first.

So roll up roll up it's time to dive into the murky world of work and swim through the floating debris to collect the bits and pieces you will need for your Personal Survival Kit.

A is for Awareness
Understanding the business world

When you cook a meal you are aware of the kitchen around you. The spicy smells that waft up your nose, the steam clouding the window and the need to avoid scalding your hand on a hot plate. Awareness of your position within your environment protects you and helps you to make sense of the world at large. The same applies to the dynamic business environment, where it's important to know where you stand and how you fit in.

Some people have an MBA and some people think that an MBA is all you need to succeed. Some of the people belonging to both of these groups think this means they can walk on water, which unfortunately is not true. Glug, glug, glug and down they go into the abyss.

Education is worthwhile and is often under utilized in the workplace, where the volume of management learning can overwhelm all but the hardiest of students. These people, through not having a busy enough social life, spend long winter evenings reciting their 10,000 top tips for self improvement. The sad truth is that a business education does not make you bullet-proof, or indispensable, or mean that you will know exactly what to do in any given situation.

There are wise souls everywhere, who have never rubbed shoulders with a management text book, who can feel success with their finger tips. Who do not need a book to tell them that having money is good and not having it is bad. Who are not going to try walking on water because they have no wish to drown in their own arrogance.

These wise souls do not scoff their breakfast from plates glazed with snappy bon mots for deciding "Which Way Is Up", or assume that simply by having the books in their house they will become a better person through a process of literary osmosis.

They know "Which Way Is Up" by touch. They can shut their eyes, breath deeply and smell the bullshit wafting in from the Crisply Shirted Ones (who always know the price of learning, but not the value of experience). They know a bit and they use that bit.

Aesop tells the fable of a Raven who wanted a drink of water, but who could not reach his beak far enough into the jar. He thought about it and then dropped in some large stones to raise the water level, clever bird.

It worked and he had a drink, but the Seagull he reported to wasn't impressed. After all, the Raven could have chipped the jar. This would have then required a maintenance Jackdaw with a tube of super glue to repair it and a form to complete in triplicate.

And the moral of the story?

Doing things requires a bit of risk.

Sadly, in our modern world the creative birds are often tagged as dangerous types, who like to think too much. They actually want to try new things and experiment, which spells danger to those bosses who cannot face up to their own inadequacies. Bosses, who despite having a head full of books, do not have the wit to laugh and learn. Bosses who stamp on those who get in their way. Those dullards who prefer to live in the land of pseudo-progress, where everything is twilight and where the shadows hang long over their own fears.

Now for those people who do not have a gilt-edged piece of cardboard with the words MBA written on it, here is an all-you-ever-need-to-know guide about business. And if you do have an MBA, here is some revision.

There are a few fundamental principles in business that have held true since Cleopatra took advantage of an ancient buyone-get-one-free offer on asses milk.

First, a business must have cash to spend.

No cash means not paying the suppliers or the employees and not paying these people is bad. Very bad. Pretending that business debts don't exist does not make them go away. If you shut your eyes, the monsters who live under the corporate bed will still get you and being hungry meat-eating monsters, who order large fries at every opportunity, the business will be gobbled up like a sneaky snack they can much between meals without losing their appetite. Most businesses who fail simply run out of cash. Like an expensive car stranded on the hard shoulder, they may have electric everything and a solar powered sunroof, but cash is like petrol. You need it.

Secondly, a business must make a profit.

The Dotcoms who surged and splurged so spectacularly are indications of the truth of this statement. In medieval times, alchemists tried to make pure gold by mixing together weird concoctions of non-gold bearing substances. Now then (and you will laugh at this) they never ever managed to produce gold. Eventually some smartass with a smattering of chemistry proclaimed that to get gold out you needed to have some traces of gold to start with. He then demonstrated this to a shocked audience and overnight shares in the alchemy business went down the garderobe.

Similarly, the dotty Dotcoms worked very hard to squeeze a profit from business plans with the gold content of a slice of lemon. If people don't want your services and you cannot make some money on the deal, then no amount of glitzy marketing is going to save your barking mad enterprise.

However, in this case the joke has been at the expense of all those people whose pension funds were invested in these modern get-rich-quick schemes. Oh dear. Three hundred years ago we could have rounded up the idiots responsible for the mess, called them all witches and burned them at the stake. Instead, we have had to avoid the backwash from the market turmoil caused by the sudden arrival and even more sudden departure of these corporate fantasies that had the longevity of a soap bubble.

Thirdly, a business must have sustainability.

Not until next week, mind you. It needs to flap its little businessy wings and make it all the way from Europe to the winter breeding grounds in Africa. Then it has to fly back for the summer months, without drowning, losing its way, or bumping into high voltage electricity cables. Sustainability means having a constant supply of willing customers, having a clear marketing strategy to plot the route ahead and having enough corporate energy to keep the wings flapping through bad weather and high winds.

All businesses must have cash and profits and sustainability. The other things you could add to the list are really just strips of wallpaper, which look pretty, but don't contribute to holding up the walls of your house.

Remember the story of the three little piggies who went into property?

The first little piggy had an MBA, but no practical experience, so he built his house out of straw. It looked like a house and it kept the rain out. He even employed a design consultant to choose the curtains. The wolf, who did not have an MBA, simply blew it down. He had blown down other straw houses before and lacked any fashion sense. Oops.

The second little piggy had been on a few courses and knew all the latest management jargon. Anxious not to go the same way as his straw-loving cousin, he invested in some fancy brochures to promote his new venture and with the money left over built a two-storey cabin made from wood. Unfortunately, dear piggy forgot to check out his adversary and failed to spot that the wolf smoked cigars, which he lit with a special forces wind-proof flame thrower. The wolf torched the place and had oak smoked roast pork for a week. Yummy.

The third little piggy felt sad that he did not have any formal business qualifications and he wondered if he was really cut out for the property development business. He already knew some things about house building by watching the other two piggies and he realized that the wolf would eventually run out of pork and come back to look for more. So he saved up and built a farm out of bricks, where he raised his own pigs and sold them for a huge profit. Eventually, he was so successful he franchised the idea and bought a yacht. When he retired, the local wolf community gave him the freedom of the town. They even made him an honorary wolf, as a mark of respect and invited him to a celebration barbeque. This little piggy was smart enough not to go. Hooray!

There is a fourth fundamental element in business, which is easy to overlook.

As easy to overlook as the assumption that, when you flick on a light switch dollops of electricity will surge through the wires to produce white light. Or, that when you stand under your power-shower the water will be fresh and clean and hot.

The fourth element is you and the foxy feline in Finance. Even the loathsome scumbag in Personnel. The fourth element is people.

Tall people. Short people. Wide people. Thin people. Young people. Old people. Business needs them all. They all have something positive to offer.

Despite the best efforts of people to invent things to get rid of everyone, the people refuse to go away. Ironic isn't it that despite some creative treachery to replace our essential functions with a computer programme, or an electronic sign, or a tiny tick-box on a website, we are still needed in the workplace?

Many years ago, when starting out as a fluffy fledgling, one of my first jobs was the office runt (silly me, the management trainee) in a sprawling company which had people and machinery scattered across an old and forbidding site. The role came complete with a wobbly chair, a desk without any functioning drawers and a prime location in the centre of the office. Smack in the middle of the jet-stream, which cut you in half whenever the outside door was opened. Seven of us crammed into the office and we passed the time between pay cheques working hard on essential top-level things. And stuff. Some of it was top-level stuff as well.

Stuff and things. My word, we were industrious.

Our days involved studying detailed reports, discussing performance figures and using our best biros to tick off the items to be issued from the warehouse. We had a dumb terminal each. And a telephone each. Mobile phones hadn't been invented yet, but we did have a different miracle machine on hand and were totally connected techno-dudes.

Okay, so the machine-of-wonder was a short jog down an outside staircase, past the speeding fork-lift-trucks, across the road, through the luxury swing doors and past the reception desk. Then head through another swing door, turn left and there it was, sitting snugly in the corner of the main office. Sandwiched between the grim recesses of the personnel department and next to the pretty petty cash clerks, was our prize.

A fax machine.

In fact the only fax machine.

To share between 200 people. What luxury!

Oh yes, we had it all. We even had an office secretary, who was terrific at making bucket loads of milky coffee, whether you wanted a "hot drinkie" or not.

This particular office was closed a long time ago. I wonder why?

The secretary was the first to go, followed by the chief buyer. A couple of days later the assistant buyer and the contracts manager were zapped and never seen again and then one of the production planners mysteriously vanished without trace (probably lost at sea, somewhere between the office and the fax machine).

The office descended into a dusty gloom, with only one other experienced planner and the management trainee to man the fort and rebel borders. Our senior management decided to play fair and not reduce the workload. They were keen to avoid us getting bored, which was sweet of them.

So the two of us sat down and worked out the best way

to survive the daily onslaught. For the next six months we battled furiously, our biros worn down to tiny stubs by frenzied ticking. Our telephone-ears glowed red with the time spent negotiating deliveries and fending off the sales department, whom people generally regarded as a bunch of lazy lounge lizards, to be treated with the same affection as free-loading neighbours who overstay their welcome.

On sunny days we managed a few essential trips to the fax machine, to enjoy the thrill of operating new technology, but that was a rare joy in our brave new world.

Then three things happened.

First, I called one of the senior managers a stupid bastard.

Not to his face of course, that would have been rude. No, at least he was only standing behind me when I said it. Phew!

Why did the terrible words tumble out? Who knows, but being young and stupid I rubbed salt into the wound by fulminating about his lack of imagination and general penchant for deploying bully boy tactics to keep us in line. It was an accurate, but unhelpful pen portrait of his managerial style and when I turned round and caught his eye, my stomach pulled on its swimming trunks and leapt off the high board.

The second thing was a real surprise.

A few days later I happened to be walking past his office when he picked up the telephone receiver and bellowed into it at the top of his voice. He couldn't see me, so I eavesdropped and it soon became clear that despite the tirade, he was very nervous. A short, stocky chap, like a grizzly bear in a suit, he had a reputation for shooting first and asking questions later, so his nervousness caught my attention.

He appeared to be yelling at a technician, but if he was so cross, why had he not stomped down to the engineering office to slap on the nipple clamps and interrogate the hapless junior face to face?

Something about the words, the volume and the anger were all mixed up. Was he really being himself? I had always assumed that, as a senior manager, he was the ruthless, cutthroat captain of our pirate ship. But was he really? Then I caught sight of a silver picture frame on his desk.

Two little smiling faces peeked out at Daddy.

So, he was not a complete bastard all the time. Out there someone had married him and had willingly produced two beautiful children. Hmmm … feelings of sympathy welled up from deep inside my cynical young heart. That wasn't meant to happen. He was supposed to be from the dark side, a management villain, trained in the black arts of keeping us in our place and getting people to jump through flaming hoops.

Perhaps he hadn't been raised by wolves? Perhaps something or someone else was stressing him? Perhaps he wasn't so different after all.

I hurried on, in case he noticed my presence and fed me to the office shredder.

After all, bears still shit in the woods, don't they?

A few weeks later the third thing happened.

I lost my job.

This is technically inaccurate because I didn't actually misplace it. It was removed from my grasp. Picture the scene:

"Oh my God! What have I done? I had my job a minute ago. It was right here. And I put it down on the desk next to the shredder and now it's gone. I only went to get a coffee. Oh shit, oh shit. Aarghh! It's gone into the shredder! I've shredded my job! I'm such an idiot..." (tears and sobbing.)

It's funny the words we use, but there's an important point here. When we say "I've lost it" we automatically assume responsibility and we rob ourselves of a bit of power to rationalize the situation.

Often we are not totally culpable for this outcome, so it can help us to stop this negative style and replace it with something more useful. The next time you're tempted to say "I've lost my job", replace the words with something like this: "That job has now ended and I'm looking forward to the next one."

My Lords and Masters were very nice about it, though. My direct boss, who wasn't the senior manager, couldn't look me in the eye. He said how sorry he was for me to be leaving and how he had tried to move me into the computer department, but sadly there was no room for someone with my biro wielding skills.

Apparently they wanted people with high foreheads who could crunch numbers and converse in geek-speak. My ability to tick important things on lists was just not good enough. The cheek of it!

That is the stomach churning thing about the fourth element. Organizations always need people, but sometimes they don't need *you*. Sometimes they do not need the brand of stuff that you are offering and sometimes they cannot afford to keep you on. You are superfluous to requirements. You are out.

However, we often lose sight of the reverse of this, which is that sometimes we don't want to sell our brand to them. Sometimes there is a better deal to be had with a different customer, who won't haggle about the price so much and who would even be grateful for our services. Always remember that there are times when no matter what their opinions about us are, we don't need them. The world is full of opportunity.

So, fuck 'em.

I evolved and found another job. It was scary at first. I had a few sleepless nights and fax machine withdrawal symptoms, but I went cold turkey and sweated through them. A few weeks later the effort was rewarded and a shiny new job was mine. After all, I had responsibilities; there were bottles of beer and cartons of cigarettes to stock up on and because my new job paid me considerably more money, my store cupboard was soon overflowing with strong German lager and expensive French smokes.

There was another bonus bounding my way as well.

In the company that booted me out, our little gang of junior management types would often retreat to the canteen. Not the one next to the loading dock though, where the evil eyes belonging to the supervisor were permanently locked on to you. She was rumoured to moonlight as a missile guidance system and her scanners revolved constantly.

No. We would scamper off to the place where all the oily types would take their break and set up our camp in the canteen in the bowels of the building. Once settled in, we would proceed to hold an emergency management meeting. These always took the form of furious smoking, drinking overpriced machine coffee and trying hard not to incinerate plastic hotdogs in the industrial-strength microwave. No one kept any minutes, because no one brought any paper.

During the course of these worthwhile discussions we would bitch and moan about the company and some of its more ludicrous policies, but would all agree that despite the hardships and petty inequalities, we loved the people. We loved being part of such a great team and that's why we stayed. Not for the money, the job satisfaction, or the opportunity to take home useful packaging products "for testing", it was for the people. We liked each other. We were a cosy clan. Then when I had no choice and was forced to find a new place to park my junior briefcase, all those comrades were left behind.

But wait, what's this? My new office was full of fine people. Warm welcoming ones, who were fun to be with and supportive of my efforts. Wow! There were good people living within more than one business! This was a revelation and did I feel like the class jackass? You bet.

Don't kid yourself.

Be aware of your environment. Stop and take a hard look at yourself and the folks around you. What's happening? Is it great? Or is it all falling apart? Are you really happy? Really? Do you know what happiness is?

Here's a tip. Think about your working life over the last six months. Which bits did you enjoy? Which bits did you really get fired up about? It doesn't matter if they were small or inconspicuous. To you they are all that matter.

They are like precious little diamonds. If they were real you would set them in a ring and show them to your closest friends. These are Diamond Days of fulfilment. They were forged on the days when you raced home, threw open the front door and shouted:

"Hi Honey, I'm home! I had a great day today! Dump the tuna salad 'cos we're dining on wild sex tonight!"

How did you feel on those Diamond Days? Chock full of good humour, energy and enthusiasm? Did your boss compliment you?

Boss
Well Maun, you did a real peachy job there. Even I, your greatest critic and source of personal abuse, marvelled at the success you just pulled off. And to think I had you down as a brain dead no-hoper!

Me
Thank you kind Sir! (Snivel, grovel, tug forelock.)

In terms of awareness you need to be aware of the tasks that you find really fulfilling. The chances are that you will live to a ripe old age so you might as well enjoy an interesting and worthwhile working life, but you do have to choose this option though. You can also choose to skimp this question and if you do, my suggestion is that you close the book, bugger off and watch television. Or play golf, or tennis, or hose down the kids' hamster. Or whatever it is you do to unwind.

You are not going to evolve. Not for a bit longer. Sorry about that.

Please take some time to reflect on the last six months. Which days were your Diamond Days? Which ones filled your heart with satisfaction and wellbeing? They may not even be days spent at work. Which other tasks really lit your fire?

When did you crack open a bottle of Chateaux Paint Stripper, the '87 vintage, and pleasured your partner on the front lawn until the sun rose and you were both caught naked by the postman? And you didn't care less about your reputation as an upstanding citizen.

Which bits would you really like to do more of, if only you had the chance?

It doesn't matter one tiny little bit, if your answers sound silly, frivolous or unachievable. It is your life. You are worth it and you are smart enough to do something about it if you really want to.

At the very least be truthful. You owe it to yourself.

❗ Please let your mind wander over the
last few months. Flick through your
● diary if that helps. Think about the
tasks that gave you a buzz. Note down the
things that first come to mind and then
when you are happy with your answers,
please turn to the very back of the book to
your Personal Survival Kit* and complete
Diamond Days of Fulfilment (page 199).
Capture the things you really enjoy doing
and remember how good you felt at the
time.

Consult the postman if you need help
with fine details.

Remember that your Kit will be
completed as you read through the rest
of the book, so you may prefer to read on
before filling in all those other tempting
blank spaces.

There is a spin off to this exercise. Look again at the
tasks or activities you have written down. Contained within
them is the secret to being a successful person at work. To
be successful all you need to do is to play to your strengths.
To do this you need to be aware of your strengths. And you
do know them, if you're honest with yourself.

In a difficult situation it makes no sense to play to your weaknesses, although a surprising number of us do. Why is this? If we are smart, why do we do dumb things?

We do things because we are stressed. Here is a scene familiar to many people:

---

* Let's pause a moment. At the back of this book is a Personal Survival Kit and throughout the book we will stop occasionally. This is so that you can spend some time thinking and can complete the PSK section by section.

Boss

Look here Maun, I'm fed up with your persistent lateness. It has been reported to me by the office sneak that you have arrived for work two minutes late every day and that on one occasion you were a full 21 minutes and 21 seconds late. (Sneaks are such sticklers for detail.)

Me

Sorry Sir. I will promise to make sure I arrive at work on time in the future.

Boss

Not good enough. I like people who can start at 7.30 am sharp every day.

Me

But the office doesn't open until 9.00 am Sir.

Boss

I know, but you need to show willing Maun. I don't like slackers on my squad.

Me

Fair enough. (Thinks: You miserable little shit.)

For me, getting to work on time is just really difficult. It's not one of my strong points. And having lived through the pain of the above scenario, history tells me that I will turn up on time for one day and then gradually slip back into my old ways. I know that as an adult I should be able to programme myself to do things differently, but this is one routine that my subconscious refuses to let some computer nerd get his grubby hands on. Perhaps it's a small act of rebellion to turn up late, or simply that to function properly

I need to pander to my night-owl tendencies. It's probably a bit of both.

However, I'm now aware of my strengths and know that one of them is stamina at work. Let's replay the scenario as it actually happened the second time around, after I had dialled in to my strengths:

Friend of Boss

Hello Maun, I'd like to talk to you about your timekeeping.

Me (smiling)

Yes?

Friend of Boss

Yes, I've been told that you are always a few minutes late for work. Is this true?

Me (smiling)

Yes it is.

Friend of Boss

Oh. It is unacceptable for a new Manager to set a poor example. You really should be here at least 15 minutes early, to show willing.

Me

But my contract clearly states that I only get paid between 9.00 am and 5.30 pm. Perhaps you would like to consider setting up some sort of flexi-time to avoid future problems?

Friend of Boss

Er, what do you mean, Maun?

Me

Well Sir, since I work an hour late most nights and given that I have had only one full lunch hour in the last three months, perhaps we should do it differently?

Friend of Boss

Er no, that won't be necessary. That will set a dangerous precedent.

Me

Okay then, I'll try harder to arrive at work on time and will try harder to have a whole hour for lunch and leave on time. Agreed?

Friend of Boss

Er, yes. I think so.

Me

Good. Thank you for bringing it to my attention. Is there anything else you would like to discuss?

Friend of Boss

No.

And I did try to arrive on time. It lasted a day, but nobody ever criticized me again for being late. I knew my strengths and used the knowledge to avoid having my arm twisted into making a hollow promise.

Working on a weakness is dead time when you could be playing to a strength. When you do work on a weakness you'll be demoralized and have to pedal twice as hard to stand still. Work on your strengths and let your successes fill your personal piggy bank of pride. You can cash in the chips later when you need to stride up corporate mountains or leap tall buildings in a single bound.

Athletes already know this. They train hard to be the fastest person in a race or the most adroit basketball player. They do not waste their time and energy (because it is a waste) trying to improve a weakness. They know what they are good at and they do not deviate from following their best skill-path. Imagine what fun the Olympics would be if the athletes and their events were matched by some sort of lottery. People would be appalled and say things like:

"This is absurd, I can't swim. I'm a gymnast." Or "How can I be expected to play table tennis, when all I packed was a horse for the Three-day Eventing?"

Olympic athletes know their strengths and hone them to perfection. They have no time to mess about.

If your Diamond Days of fulfilment happened whenever you made a business presentation, then it is a fair bet that you have excellent communication skills. If you completed a complex project on time and to budget and felt enriched by the experience, then project management is a natural strength.

Can you juggle? Or make people laugh? You can probably do both. If you hate your job and want to be a circus clown, then write it down.

> **❗ Sit quietly and reflect on your key
> strengths or talents, which are part of
> ● the work you did on your Diamond
> Days. Everybody is good at something.
> Then turn to the back of the book and
> write them down in your PSK.**

> **What is really special about you? What
> talents do you have that, no matter what
> your boss thinks about you, he always
> asks you to use? The bastard probably
> won't lift a finger to help you through a
> crisis, but he does know your strengths.
> Be honest with yourself and complete
> Harvest my Strengths (page 200).**

Once you have written them down say them out loud. This
will make them come alive and dance like fireflies before
your eyes. Tell your best friends what your strengths are.
They will agree and make you feel even better.

There is nothing wrong in being a bit bombastic at
times. If you are not going to champion your own talents
why the hell should anyone else do it for you? Dig out your
old cheerleading pom-poms and dance up and down in
front of the neighbours chanting:

"2-4-6-8-Who do we appreciate? Me!"

A is for awareness.

A genuine awareness of your working environment.
Awareness of the fact that your personal horizons can sweep
on past the office door.

Awareness of the essential bits every business has to have
to keep it going. If the business has lost or broken them,
you will need to face up to the fact that changes must be
made to recover the position. These changes may not be in

your favour, so don't stick your head in the sand. That will only tempt someone to kick you up the ass.

Remember that you can choose whom to market your own brand of stuff to. Go for the customers who will buy your pitch and who will not attempt to chip you on price.

Be aware of those tasks which fill you with a strong feeling of fulfilment. Doing more of these can really help to give your career a boost, as you will find yourself feeling more satisfied with your work and your boss will tend to appreciate your contribution much more.

Cherish your Diamond Days and play to your strengths.

And most of all, above everything; don't lie to yourself.

You only have one life, so make it an honest one. You're too smart to pull the wool over your own eyes.

04

B is for Behaviour
What do you actually do?

It's all about behaviour. Personality is like your face. There are certain features on your face, which you have had from an early age. Your eyebrows sprouted into nestling bushes, your nose popped out into its distinctive shape and your ears unfurled themselves like two solar panels on a spy satellite. Despite the softening of the years and the odd grey hair your face is pretty well fixed. Your behaviour is what you do with your face. Do you smile? Do you frown? Do you wear dark glasses all the time?

In the working environment, we are judged by our behaviour. A constant stream of actions and reactions, behaviour covers all the things that our bodies do and our mouths say.

A strong performance will cause people to overlook poor behaviour, but the moment you miss the target or a touchy decision has to be taken, your performance will take a back seat to your behaviour.

People join companies and leave managers. The flip side of this is that bosses hire hope and dispose of despair.

They hope your performance in the role will beat your sparkling performance at the assessment centre and that the psychometric profile you completed was right on the money. A good tip is not to attempt to cheat on these exercises, however odious you find them. Try and be smart with your answers and the resulting profile will instantly have you pegged as a cross between a baboon and a marmoset. Don't go there, unless you're after a career in zoology.

Bosses hope that you will turn up to work sober and primed for action, work diligently and manage to avoid stealing their possessions or their customers. They keep their fingers crossed that you will say complimentary things about them when touring the world on their behalf. Living in dreary hotels far away from your family and loved ones (if these two support groups are not the same), feasting on highly processed saturated fats and drinking carbonated battery acid.

They hope you will work hard, avoid threatening them and stick around until they choose to dispose of you. They hate it when you muck up their nasty little plans for your career non-development by baling out, or by allowing yourself to be seduced by the bright lights of a competitor.

Bosses dispose of despair.

They can smell the funereal air of a Self-Fulfilling Prophecy (SFP) from ten miles and they just hate the stench of rotten eggs under their nose. Becoming an SFP is a fast track to the outside world and you will slide out quicker than a speed skater with a rocket pack.

A Self-Fulfilling Prophecy happens when you exhibit inappropriate behaviour and then deny its existence when someone holds up a mirror. You actively contribute to your own downfall by doing nothing to help yourself and instead simply fret and say:

"I think I'm going to be sacked."

This incisive insight is legitimized by the stinking line:

"Nothing can be done."

Which is a big skip load of grade-A industrial rubbish.

And the one who makes up the rules on this is your dear boss, because it's his perception that counts. His perception of your behaviour is all that matters. Your own views are as inconsequential as the small bug you flattened on the drive to work.

Rule number one is that keeping to his rules is essential.

This may be a chuffing nuisance, but it's not a legitimate excuse for not playing the game.

Two people I knew fell prey to the curse of the Self-Fulfilling Prophecy and on both occasions they lost their jobs and were virtually carried out of the building, protesting their innocence and hurling abuse at the personnel manager.

Treating personnel managers to a selection of tart comments is a good tonic, although not overly constructive. However, given that a large percentage of them are cold, flint-hearted individuals who scrape out a dingy existence in the shadows at the edge of the corporate stage, they can take it. People have ambitions to become astronauts, train drivers or statesmen. People end up as personnel managers.

The real down side to becoming a Self-Fulfilling Prophecy is that it can become all consuming. Once at home and staring at the walls, an overwhelming sense of injustice can bite you, like a poisonous spider and paralyze your limbs for days. You slob out, watch daytime television on your wide screen media centre and pout like a petulant child who refuses to go outside and enjoy the sunshine.

How could they have chucked you out? Weren't you the key team player responsible for manning the paper clip dispenser? How are they going to survive when the paper clips run out? The trouble is they will. This is both shocking and true. The sad truth is that you really had to go before your bitter attitude spread sour discontent to the rest of the organization. But do not despair, some things are simply not meant to be.

Our lives are all bolted together from a series of steep spiral staircases, surprising doglegs and slippery helter-skelter rides. Everyone has turbulent patches to cope with and everyone gets a few dents in their personal bodywork.

You can choose to mope, or you can choose to do something positive and move on in your life. More mature people reflect on their experience and then choose to behave like an adult: with dignity and thoughtfulness.

Respond to your present circumstances in a purposeful and measured way.

Get a grip. Take a breath. Try the first step.

If the path ahead seems to stretch into the distance and taunts you to give up before taking a single stride, do not let yourself be overwhelmed by the challenge. Instead, concentrate on taking small steps until you get the feel of the twists and turns.

Remember that your strengths have not evaporated overnight. You are still smart and are still needed. Probably needed by the jerk that just bounced you out, but that's his problem. You'll get over it, but he may not.

When our behaviour becomes an irritation to our boss, we instantly cross the line from being a productive and useful employee to an expensive albatross. To him we become a big fat bird who keeps crapping on his time and his future.

Here's an exercise to consider.

Next time you're inside a department store march up to the perfume counter and experiment with the different smells on offer. No one will shoot you for doing this, but you'll see that some odours suit you, whilst others make your nose wrinkle and probably the nose of the glamorous sales assistant too. The one with the inch-deep crust of pancake foundation that could double up as a pizza base.

Think of crossing that thin line from "productive" to "albatross" as the act of trying the perfume which doesn't suit you. When it's safely in the bottle no one minds, but once you have tried it on the smell is distasteful. Bad smells have tremendous staying power and even after scrubbing several times a faint trace can cause trouble.

Back in the office there's now a stink on the loose. You're vinegar. You could take some steps to help the situation by masking the smell with strong perfume, or by moving your desk into the car park to bathe in fresh air.

The key point is you could do something, but unfortunately the chances are that you will not notice your boss wrinkling his nose and you'll plough on. Eventually a bell rings in your head, you finally notice the boss starting to cool towards you and fear grips your heart that something is not all rosy in The Garden of Employment.

Consequently, you over compensate and present more unwanted ideas to him. Or you attempt to ingratiate yourself by laughing at one of his pathetic bad-taste jokes, or uncharacteristically volunteer for extra duties. In short you stop behaving like your true self.

In a practical sense you are devoting more time to your weaknesses than to your strengths, to the point where people are taking bets on what your strengths really are. You test the waters by pitching speculative comments to your colleagues, such as:

"Is it me or is the boss out to get me?"

This is a really bad sign. You could talk to your boss about it, but he's not going to admit the truth, or give you a sneaky peeky at his future plans if they don't include you. He's a bastard who doesn't want to spoil his fun and despite being an omnipotent force in the business, he doesn't actually own a crystal ball and has never worked overtime as a dubious fortune teller at the local fair.

This means that there are times when he is unable to see into the future to help you out, even if he wanted to. Which he doesn't. He may have balls of glass, but kicking them is not going to win you any prizes.

Because of one small event, or a few isolated incidents, you have convinced yourself that you are for the chop and so have changed your behaviour. Except now you are making things worse because your behaviour has swung in the wrong direction. The more you do nothing, apart from seeking reassurance, the more you behave like an idiot. The more you do that, the more your boss will start to think you are an idiot, until he can stand it no more and shoves you out through the door.

And what's the first thing you say to make yourself feel better?

"My boss is a bastard."

Of course he is, and you're a vestal virgin. Not.

Take a look in the mirror and see if you've changed. If your rugged good looks have been swapped for a pair of fluffy ears and a pointy mouth then look down and check out whether you have hooves instead of feet. If your toes are now cloven and you have a swishy tail, then you've become an antelope, you dope. You are no longer a fat albatross, dropping guano on his head. You've become something much worse: a tasty meal for a hungry carnivore.

"That's a large antelope with cheese and a side order of antelope with the chilli sauce. To go."

Stop at this point and think back to an uncomfortable situation at work. One that left a bad taste in your mouth.

Or one that left you boiling and hissing, like a badly serviced steam engine.

What emotions did you feel at the time? Anger and frustration perhaps? What did you do?

- Smoke a cigarette?
- Have a drink?
- Bash in the company car?
- Smack your boss in the chops?

Now think about it again. Did you see it coming? No really, think hard. Was there a small clue signposting the future, if only a kind colleague had pointed it out to you? Could the current reality of your present situation have been altered by a timely slice of evasive action? What could have helped you out?

If your first and instant response to these questions is simply "nothing" then sniff your armpits to make sure you are not a smelly old Self-Fulfilling Prophecy.

Stuck?

For starters, think about your strengths and whether you are using them.

Have some fun by listing your ten most important task activities over the last couple of weeks. Take a clean sheet of paper and have a go. In a column next to the activities write down your top three talents and your top three weaknesses and then zoom down the list of tasks and score each one with 1 if it used a strength and a 0 if it used a weakness. Add up your final score and start weeping if it was less than

4. You need to reappraise your current career path before you're forced to walk the plank sticking over the side of the pirate ship of business.

When I did this exercise it became obvious to me that a chunk of my energy was going into a particular sales activity that was not my forte. So, after chatting with the sales manager we traded some tasks to make sure we were both playing to our strengths. We achieved more and became less stressed.

You may be surprised to learn the truth about your life at work and realize that although you're working hard, by concentrating mainly on tasks relating to weaknesses you are in fact standing still. So still, that you could be mistaken for a statue. Pigeons land on your shoulders, peck your nose, or shit on your bald patch.

It is also likely that you may have some secondary strengths languishing at the bottom of the bag and it would be a pity to write them off without giving them a few laps round the cinder track of your working life. If you have the brain of a genius, the libido of a buck rabbit and owned your own executive harem you wouldn't hire a couple of eunuchs to do the pleasuring would you? No way. Anyway, eunuchs cost money and are hard to find.

Think about what these second line strengths are and then jot them down.

You need to do the things that make you smile.

Do you take your holidays camped out on the neighbour's front lawn? Do you hell. You fly round the world and take digital pictures of ancient ruins, or swim in toxic, but exotic seas in your body hugging rubber suit.

Can you imagine how people managed when they wore knitted bathing costumes?

Probably about the same as people did when at junior school they were forced to have a crack at basic survival during swimming lessons.

This involved their overweight PE teacher trying to reduce his class size by forcing his charges to leap into the deep end of the local swimming baths wearing their pyjamas. The name of the game was to avoid drowning at all costs and amazingly all 35 in our class made it to safety. Nobody wanted to carry on doing something that was tiring them out.

We knew that and we were only little children. Could someone have helped you to stop the slippery slide? A friend, or a partner? A parent, or a colleague? A spare lover? If you're up shit creek, who could help row for you, or throw you a new paddle? Who could fish you out of the pool when you are tired of treading water in your corporate pyjamas?

! ● Pop to the back of the book, to your Personal Survival Kit and complete My Support Group (page 201). Write down the names, mobile phone numbers (more useful in a crisis) and e-mail addresses of your personal backup team and how they can support you. Who do you know

(either at work, or in your private life)
who you trust to give you sound advice
and encourage you to share your ideas
without judging you?

These people may not simply be your best
friends. If they cannot really do anything
above hold you hand, massage your back
or provide paid executive relief, then you
should scrub them off and put down
some more names. Don't confuse pleasure
with support. The first lasts momentarily,
whereas the second can change your life.
Or save it.

It's all about behaviour and fortunately you can shape yours, so all is not lost. As the dog trainer said to the lady whose ear had just been chewed off by her Doberman dog:

"Fluffy is not evil, just poorly behaved."

A short-sighted hedgehog was trying to make love to a scrubbing brush, when a passing mouse pointed out his error. The hedgehog shrugged his spiny shoulders and sighed:

"Sometimes I make mistakes, but that doesn't stop me from trying again."

The hedgehog then tried again.

"That's a broom," said the mouse, helpfully.

"I'll get there in the end," shouted the hedgehog. "So why don't you just bugger off?"

Our personality is fixed. We choose our behaviour. To make effective choices we have to learn from our mistakes and increase our repertoire of options. Our personality is hard-wired into us. Etched into our soul by a heady combination of genetics and childhood experience, gained as we explored our world and decided what fulfilled our needs, or caused us trauma. Gradually we focused on the bits we liked and which kept us safe. We soon learned to filter out the bits we disliked, or which got us bashed.

Our parents (or guardians), families and friends influenced us as well. They gave us our sense of who we are and wrinkled the edges of our personalities with their etiquette, paranoia and prejudice. How many sons support their father's football team? How many daughters grow up with their mother's views on men? All of these decisions, choices and preferences became pretty well fixed in the first few years of life.

Picture the cross-sections of rock you see on a natural history programme. They were formed from bands of sediment which built up when sea creatures died and sank gently to the bottom of the embryo oceans. Natural forces pushed up the seabed and crushed them into rocky strips which remain distinct, even after the edges have been extensively weathered by wind and rain. Our personalities are a bit like this; built on our childhood bedrock and then overlaid with accumulated deposits. The layers we have are unique to us.

Celebrate your personality and enjoy being you. Reflect on your behaviour and remember that it is often chosen for you by your subconscious.

Imagine driving a car. Part of you is watching the road for hazards and turning the wheel. Your conscious self is deciding which way to go, how fast to drive and so on. However, there are times when your subconscious will act like an in-built driving instructor. He may have once drilled a mantra into you that said something like "slow down in wet weather" and this has become instinctive. The moment it rains, you ease back slightly on the accelerator and drive on, without realizing that you had slowed down.

Behaviour requires constant monitoring. It can sneak up on you and slap you in the face. Have you ever said:

"I didn't mean to do that" Or,

"I've done that before" Or,

"Just what the hell happened there?"

If you haven't said any of these, then you're a lying loser. Stop right now and check to make sure you haven't turned into an antelope, you dope.

My own behaviour monitoring began after completing a serious-minded outdoor management training course. This was a great use of time. We were trained to carry barrels over "mine fields", solve complex problems with knotted ropes and work as a team with a wide spectrum of the company's management hierarchy. Most of whom had never been seen anywhere near our office and weren't about to change old habits on the basis of one crappy course. Still, it passed the time and for me it was a revelation.

The highlight was a trip to a local set of caves, which despite being tamer than a hand reared baby sparrow, still made the group fall silent when the daylight petered out and our boots began to slosh in ankle deep water. We splashed about for a time, then climbed into a side passage and followed it, first crouching and then down on our hands and knees as the roof closed in and the walls funnelled us into an ever tighter herd.

Eventually we all bumped into each other and when the log jam started to give people the jitters our instructor pointed to a slender crack in the floor, the size of a letter box, and said, in that casual instructory way such people have:

"Right team, we can only reach the next section by dropping down through this hole."

This instantly prompted a barrage of worried shouts and well-rounded team building comments, such as:

"You must be joking."

"I'm calling my lawyer." And…

"Sod off."

However, despite our reservations we all made it through with unexpected ease and slid into a waist-high stream, that filled our boots with ice cold water and made walking a novel and squishy experience.

We sloshed onwards and eventually emerged into the sunlight, blinking like moles and feeling very pleased with ourselves.

Full of self-confidence at surviving the cave, I omitted to remember the behavioural lessons about team discipline and self-control and so managed to blow a large hole in my personal credibility by spitting my dummy out on the next exercise.

Dried and changed and back at the ranch we had to defuse a dangerous pretend bomb with a piece of string and a safety pin. This was scary stuff requiring a delicate touch and a rudimentary understanding of the principles of gravity. The lads back in the office would doubtless be reassured that the quality audit due next week would be in safe hands now I could draw them a wiring diagram of a milk bottle.

Unfortunately, my team for the exercise consisted largely of engineers, who would insist on trying to figure it out by relying on their intimate knowledge of bodging all things electrical. Having seen something similar on a television quiz programme I knew the answer and told them so a number of times, even supporting my case with helpful team building language, such as:

"Listen to me you morons. Could the person with their brain switched on please stick a hand in the air?"

Needless to say they were immuned to my charms.

After a final attempt to convince them of the one true answer, I puckered up and spat out my dummy.

"Do it your way then," I shouted.

"Good luck," I added.

Fail miserably, I meant.

They did, but during the debrief I copped for it,

because they had misinterpreted my suggestions and advice as hectoring and shouting. Never!

That was an unpleasant surprise and the instructor made it crystal clear that just by doing the course without any follow-up work, my behaviour would not change for longer than 30 seconds. Apparently, you needed to learn the lessons and use such experiences as touchstones to refer back to on a regular basis. I decided to learn from my mistake.

Time passed and eventually a second course rolled up, with a different bunch of colleagues. Determined not to chuck my toys out of the pram, I gave myself a lecture in stern tones about how I would maintain a serene and calm exterior and provide only sensible advice and productive comments to the group at large.

First day. First exercise. First ten minutes.

That's all I lasted before my dummy flew a good ten feet and off I stomped for a sulk. I thought I was being reasonable to let the group leader put his useless plan into action. After all, it wasn't my fault if he was a sponge-brained invertebrate, with all the decisiveness and flair of a garden snail.

Sometimes, despite a bit of learning we can still get caught out.

We are not robots. We are thinking, feeling people who react to each other and get tripped up by the raised corner of one of our emotional paving slabs. Life is like that really, so there's no point tearing your heart out over occasional mistakes. Apologize to people. Laugh about it and move on. People will respect you for this.

Let humility become one of your greatest weapons.

When you make a mistake at work it is so tempting to suggest it was "circumstance" or "the receptionist" who caused the problem, when you know all along that you were the culprit. Your colleagues know too because, not only are they not stupid, they can also smell the cow pat under your desk, steaming away guiltily.

People who wave away their own mistakes as if they were bad cooking experiences, caused by a faulty oven, quickly destroy their colleagues' trust in them. If you make a mistake, then own up to it and people will admire your honesty and integrity. A side effect is that you will not have to walk round the office with a craven look plastered on your face and instead will be able to smile and enjoy the rest of your day. Everybody makes mistakes, so don't kid yourself that you're Mr or Ms Perfect.

We always value the presence of an honest person in our midst.

Reflecting on my training experiences, I did choose to sulk. I could have spoken less sharply to the leader and perhaps encouraged him to have a practice attempt at his solution. I could have caught my dummy and apologized on the spot for undermining his position. I could even have listened to what he was trying to say.

Listening is a key skill that requires constant practice.

It's a bit like trying to master the intricacies of a bit of Bach on the ukulele. It takes time, dedication and a willingness to improve. All decent relationships are built on a foundation of active listening. This does not mean writing whilst someone is talking to you, trying to butt in with your comments, or wiggling your ears like an Indian elephant with a twitch.

You are not Julius Caesar about to address the Senate on an important matter of state, so avoid the temptation to wave an imperial hand to attract attention when someone is talking. Next time a rude individual holds up one of their hands in a meeting, fix them with a sincere stare and say:

"Thank you, I'll have a coffee. Two sugars."

Good listeners maintain eye contact, don't play with pens, scratch their crotches or butt in with their own comments. If you are listening to yourself thinking, then you are not listening to the other person. Write down your thoughts, to avoid losing them and then pay attention. Poor listening is poor behaviour and can really piss people off, so take a moment to think about which bad habits you could get rid of.

Think back to the time when you last slid up to the painted lovelies in your local watering hole, strapped into their slinky evening gowns and propped against the bar. Remember the superb listening skills you harnessed when you attempted to ingratiate yourself into their lives and hopefully past their underwear?

Clearly then, you have a reservoir of good listening skills on board. You just need to find the right incentive to tap into them.

Improving your listening skills will improve your powers of observation, which is an important first step when learning about yourself.

Close observation of your actions will help to develop new behaviours and one option would be to video yourself, although this is almost always impractical and not something your lover will readily agree to. Having a camera, sound gear and two arc lights in your face is not going to encourage you to behave normally. And, before you rush off to your local DIY store, a large mirror on the ceiling is not a sensible alternative. They are fine for porn movies, but not for sorting out your career, unless you already have star billing on the top shelf of your local newsagent.

The best way to observe is to ask questions and then listen to the information contained within the answers. Start your observations with the one person at work who really gets under your skin, the one who seems to lack any sense of what a complete fuckwit they really are. You probably cross swords with this person on a daily basis and the resulting sparks make both of your lives somewhat more unpleasant.

To improve things you will need to update your behaviour and not let yourself get sucked in by the same old feelings of frustration and resentment. However, as you are reading this book, and the other person is not, you will have to make the first move. Life is like that sometimes and it's no good bitching about fairness. You will simply have to roll up your corporate sleeves and get stuck in.

Think about how you interact with each other and what sort of things you say about this person to your friends. It may surprise you to learn that he will be having a mirror image conversation with his buddies and if you are convinced he is a stupid waste of space, he probably sees you as an overpowering bully.

Are you being reasonable or just plain picky? Are your comments warm and friendly, or sarcastic daisy cutters that chop his feet off? What do you think he says to his partner after yet another slugging match with you? More importantly, what does he say to your shared boss during his annual appraisal?

A junior manager complained long and loud about a colleague in the sales department, who on the face of it had no redeeming features. The sales rep did not strike the junior manager as being particularly clever, or hard working and did not seem to possess a magnetic personality, or even-handed leadership skills. He did have two redeeming features though.

First he was able to enter buildings through locked doors and slide through the tightest of cracks to deliver his sales pitch. (The mark of a true salesman.)

And secondly, he had built productive relationships with several key customers. However the junior manager, who was shot through with imperfections himself, failed to realize this. He never once questioned his own behaviour around the office, or noticed the grating effect he had on his colleagues, who became steadily less well disposed towards him. Eventually he was shown the door. What a surprise.

In these situations there is always a winner and a loser and if you don't alter your behaviour you will be the loser, because you'll need the political skills of a basking shark to win this kind of competition. Life is too short to spend time trying to defeat one person in one organization. Instead use your energy on yourself because the improvement will benefit you for much longer.

Gain an insight into your actions by asking suitably perceptive and searching reflective questions, such as:

- With whom do I cross swords?
- When do I do this?
- What does she say or do that irritates me?
- How do I respond?
- How do I feel after the conversation? Fed up with him, or cross with myself?
- How does she feel? Am I being a bully?
- What words could I use to help me?
- What could I do differently?

Doing "something differently" can include holding a proper meeting to avoid impromptu sessions in the corridor, or preparing an agenda to ensure the boundaries are clear. If you agree to a handful of achievable common objectives, do make sure they are genuinely reasonable and not forced out after putting him in a headlock, though.

Words that help are those that appeal to his personality.

If he is a thoughtful person offer him time to reflect. If he is nervous, ask him what his concerns are. If you think someone hates being told what to do then outline a few options to help them feel included in the decision making process. You can indicate your preference, but give them time to discuss the ideas you are suggesting. People like to feel they have a sense of ownership in a process. Ownership is rooted in the freedom to make some choices. People just love to make choices.

Rehearse and make notes. If someone is aggressive then prepare your comments in advance and stick to them. Rehearsal is a key tool for any situation, but it is practised with staggering irregularity.

Imagine you are a concert pianist about to give a recital in front of an excited audience of celebrities. Would you bowl up unprepared and mug through a few bars of Rachmaninov before exiting, stage left, to a howl of abuse? No, I think not.

Using appropriate language is a corner stone to developing better relationships, which in turn will help to increase your inner health.

Therefore, it's worth thinking about the actual, specific words you use. The wrong words can make you sound like a nagging parent, a hectoring bully, or a spiteful child and will get a strong reaction.

How often do you use the following words?

You should … You ought … You must … I think that you … No, but … You need … You will … Do this.

Every day? Every time you open your mouth?

These are almost always going to get you into trouble because you are telling the other person what to think, or how to behave. You have removed their power of choice and have placed them in an inferior position, which will encourage them to sulk, or be aggressive, by way of a defensive response. Remember how much *you* hated to be told to do stuff as a kid? Try replacing these tricky words with:

How ... when ... where ... why ... what ... what else ... would you consider ... I feel that ... yes and ... and if we do this we can ... please ... when you do that I feel ...

These alternatives will help you to appear assertive instead of overbearing and will reduce the likelihood of trouble. Write down the key part of your pitch to the other person and anticipate the probable response. Here is an example for you to chew over:

"I think that you should give me a new job" (Likely reply: Well I don't think I should, so bugger off.)

Instead, replace this with:

"I feel that I've outgrown my current role. Please would you listen to my suggestions and then let me have your comments in a couple of days?" (Likely reply: Hmmm, I can see you've given it some thought. I'll have a look and we can talk again.)

Naming your feelings often sounds less aggressive than a colder "I think" approach and feelings can be difficult to argue with.

In addition, the difference between "no, but" and "yes, and" can be striking.

The former is used to close conversations, or to send them down blind alleyways, whereas the latter opens up new possibilities and overcomes obstacles.

The following exchange is a classic scenario:

Boss
I would like you to write that report today. Can you do it?
Junior
No, but I could do it for you for next week.
Boss
But I need it today.
Junior
Sorry, can't be done.

Do you think Junior will have moved up the office pop charts? Try again, my son.

Boss
I would like you to write that report today. Can you do it?
Junior
Yes, *and if* you helped me to resolve these delivery issues I could have it on your desk before lunch.
Boss
Great, I'll give the Warehouse a call.
Junior
Thank you.

People often use *no, but* as a blocking tactic and your boss doesn't like to be blocked. Despite being a bastard his needs are real to him and your blocking is not helping anyone. It's simply childish behaviour that would not withstand close scrutiny.

It's amazing how many people have absolutely no time for an urgent request, but still manage to squeeze in a quick gossip by the water cooler. You may feel that you have won a small victory, but you're wrong and will lose out when tough decisions have to be taken.

Do not underestimate the effect of a positive, mature response. You will feel better and you will make those around you feel better. Your enthusiasm will grow and your inner health will puff out its chest.

When trying to put together a more fulfilling life for yourself, keep using *yes and* or *and if* to keep opening up new possibilities. A loser's view is like this: "I would like to run my own business, but I don't have any money". The end.

Whereas a learner's view is more like this: "I would like to run my own business *and if* I visited the bank they may lend me some money *and if* I asked my friends they may also help me *and if* they were concerned I could sell them shares to show that I was after a loan and not a gift *and if* they helped me I would be able to pay them back double *and if* I did all these things I would be able to fulfil an ambition and be happy and enjoy myself and … and … and."

Now you're cooking.

The trick is to make the first response to a question: *Yes, and …*

And! Could you do something? Yes. And if you did it like that could you do something else as well? Could you fly to the moon? Yes, and if you start planning now you will beat the winter weather.

Keep asking yourself lots of reflective questions to open up your mind to the reality of the situation and your self-knowledge will soon accumulate. Make diary notes of key insights, to make sure your new learning is not lost. People often find that understanding their own behaviour is a slippery concept and, like a bar of soft soap, it can be difficult to get a grip of. To help overcome this, here are two suggestions for you to noodle over:

The first is to ask your spouse, partner or casual weekend lover how you handled a situation which they are familiar with. They will usually be honest and open with you. Your job is to laugh and learn. And if you avoid asking them when you're both entwined in a deeply sticky romantic moment, you'll get some useful information. Timing is everything.

The second is to keep a note of a sour conversation. Stick it to the door of your fridge and next morning, when munching nourishing flakes of chipboard, read it and think of one thing you would have done differently if you could start over. One thing you could have changed, not one thing the other person could have done. It's always up to you to make the first move.

B is for behaviour.

It's all about behaviour, whether we smile or frown, act or react. We need to be self-aware to avoid becoming the office albatross or an antelope shaped Self-Fulfilling Prophecy.

We have to be observant to become self-aware.

We can build up our personal credibility by slathering ourselves in the moisturizing benefits of humility.

Soak up information by deploying your active listening skills and use this as a foundation to start building up a detailed portrait of yourself in the office.

Once you have a handful of rough observations start to develop new ways of approaching tired old situations, to help resolve long-standing conflicts and to ensure your limited energies are being spent on developing yourself.

The important thing is to find a way to learn which works for you. Then smile to yourself and choose a small chocolate flavoured reward for surviving each situation in a positive and healthy way.

Use appropriate language and focus on those words and actions that will contribute to a successful outcome. Kick out the ones that get you punched. Write things down and rehearse them, because even gifted piano players have to practise for hours each day.

Personality is fixed, behaviour is a choice. Choose wisely.

And next up we meet our little friend.

05

E is for Ego
The little sod inside us all

On numerous occasions, people have commented that I have an *ego*. Well, no shit, Sherlock. We all have egos, but unfortunately some people have decided that having one is a bad thing and they don't want it, which is like saying:

"I don't need my spleen today, so I've left it behind in the fridge."

Such types hold the unshakeable opinion that people with "egos" have scary tattoos and are dangerous, in the same way that biker dudes in leathers are all going to spit roast innocent grandmothers over an open fire. Biker dudes would never do that to sweet little old ladies. They only spit roast hippies, who generally deserve it.

However, the people who are really dangerous and should be dealt with firmly are those who put others down by saying things like:

"She has an ego."

By logical extension their next sentence should be:

"And I am a thoughtless moron with a wing nut for a brain."

We all have egos, dummy.

Your ego can be your best friend and whistle up some adrenaline to get you out of a scrape. Or it can be your personal nemesis and trample on your daisies. Your ego is like a little jumping bean who surfs on your desires. All the time he is standing on the sandy beach of your subconscious waiting for the next big wave to break, jumping up and down excitedly and grinning at the sea.

Picture him, in his little wetsuit with his surfboard planted in the sand. Waxed, glistening and ready for action.

The more he jumps and shouts with excitement the bigger the waves grow. It's almost as if he is responsible for making the waves swell into dangerously exciting walls of foaming white water.

Which, of course, he is.

The highest wave starts to peak. He grabs his board and speedily paddles out to be in position before it breaks. In a flash he is up and surfing.

He is the Surf King.

He is the coolest bean on the water, with the biggest bulge in the tightest trunks. And then the wave breaks over him, shoots him right up to the high tide mark and dumps him, with his head stuck in a pile of seaweed. He feels a foolish bean and his bulge dwindles to a harmless nobble.

On a good day our ego will give us an adrenaline-kick that makes us perform well.

We can use it to help make that crucial presentation, win that tough sales pitch, or design a smart profit-making solution. We surf on the rolling waves and bask in the glory of the moment. We need our ego to help prod us into life, to give us a certain edge to our behaviour. This is good and healthy and productive.

In our Western culture good health is something that we assume and only treat when it goes wrong. We rush off to the doctor, or quack if you're unlucky, and demand that we receive pills and ointments, or that he uses a fabulous space age gadget to probe our innermost valves and organs. By contrast the culture in China is the reverse. Doctors focus on keeping you healthy. They work hard to prevent you from getting sick, but of course, we in the West are always right. Aren't we?

The notion of health in this context is to ensure that we are healthy through and through. Not just by getting regular exercise and a nutritious balanced diet. If you eat a shredded Hessian sack for breakfast, swill decaff coffee all day, nibble wholemeal burgers for lunch, do a job that is not fulfilling and work for an evil snake, are you healthy or not?

Health is a vital ingredient to ensure we have the energy to continue with our arduous lives. Heck, we may even have enough to enjoy ourselves! Our ego can help us to achieve good health, so don't mock him.

The trouble is that he is an adrenaline junkie and never knows when to quit.

If our little jumping bean jumps up and down too much the waves swamp him. We will be seduced by that expensive must-have executive toy, or will storm out of a meeting in a fit of pique, or refuse to accept reasonable feedback on our work issues.

Once you recognize that there is a little jumping bean inside, you can have some fun and turn his energy to your advantage. Occasionally, it is healthy to let him go surfing and give him the chance to enjoy the wind in his face, but be careful not to allow the little chap to get addicted to it.

Company cars, offices and over-developed mobile phones can all be symptoms of too much ego surfing. Are they all totally necessary?

Do you really need the leather seats and the satellite navigation to help you drive ten miles to work each morning? If you do not have the corner office will you really drop dead from shame? Your mobile is the latest model that doubles up as a thermometer and has an in-built altimeter? Very useful when you're feeling sick in a tower block and need to tell the ambulance men on which floor to step off the elevator.

There is very little that we actually need, but there is a great deal which our ego tells us we must have, and so our behaviour is driven accordingly. It can be surprising how much you possess simply because you wanted it. It was a shiny thing! I just *had* to have it!

Learn to keep a grip on your ego and hide his surfboard occasionally. Take evasive action, or use the word "no", like you do with the kids.

A useful start is to list all the non-essential purchases you have made over the last four weeks. Skip food and beer, as you have to have some sustenance in life. Was there anything you purchased that you didn't really need? That you could have lived without?

To get control over your ego means changing your behaviour. Alter your routine to avoid the sweet shop, or the boutique and if you really must exercise your credit card, make sure you are not seduced into paying extra for unwanted capacity, speed or size. How many of us have said something similar to the following:

"You know dear, the Jones's will laugh at us if we don't purchase the latest miniature home computer. The Sugar-Lump 2020. It has a massive 900 pebble hard drive, can calculate the mean temperature across three different time zones, has smart gold trim and comes with a rough-rider mouse."

Ask yourself three dazzlingly useful questions:

"Do I really need this?"

"What would I do instead?"

"What could I do differently?"

If we have a fulfilling job and the love of our family and friends, we are usually perfectly happy.

The rest is just gloss and baggage.

Decide what you can live without and what you can sacrifice.

A successful executive wanted to buy a business and decided to sacrifice her ritzy lifestyle to help finance it. She knew something had to give way to make room for the new horizons in her life. Her decision required advanced planning and involved a large element of risk and when she thought about it, she realized she could survive, without the executive trappings, whilst putting together the elements of her new career.

She persevered through numerous false starts, misleading information and the apparent fall from the executive high life. She stuck with it and is now the owner of a successful and growing business. She also knew that whilst the notion of "risk" can be unsettling, it's also an essential part of investing in the future.

Risking something is part of the deal here. By moving on in some way, you may risk having to learn new things, drive further to work each day, or develop new relationships with people. Perhaps all you will risk is upsetting the people you leave behind and perhaps if this applies to a Bastard Boss that's not so bad. Don't scare yourself though. Instead, focus on thinking about these changes as *investments* in a happier life.

Remember to consider all the little things in life as well.

Sacrificing a daily chocolate bar can have as much impact on your inner health as sacrificing a flash car. If they are *your* sacrifices they are important to you, no matter how big or small. The essential things to stock up on are love and fulfilment.

Material goods are a poor substitute, heavy to carry and need a constant source of batteries to keep them functioning.

! Please turn to your Personal Survival
Kit. Think about your oak desk, fat
● car or even fatter business lunches
and realize that these things can always
be picked up again later on. Complete
Keeping my Ego in Sight (page 202) by
noting down the main items you can
leave behind, when the time comes to
move on. Assume you will have to walk
to safety and are not able to carry a heavy
backpack. (Remember to travel light.)

What are the things that weigh you
down? What can easily be replaced at a
future date? What are you prepared to
sacrifice, or do differently, to reach new
horizons? Note down a couple of things
that you are prepared to change to help
move you towards a better working life.

It is amazing how many people, when questioned, will say
how much of a blow it was to lose their company car, which
was only ever a petrol snorting lump of metal. In itself it
did not make them happy, or mow the lawn for them, or
tell funny jokes to cheer them up in traffic jams. The cup
holders did not enrich their lives to the point where they
were given names and treated with the same affection that
the family pet enjoyed.

No, the car was a lump and way too grand, but our egos miss the hit of the big waves and jump up and down to ensure we do something to get the surf up again. Encourage your ego to forsake technological highs and concentrate on nourishing your inner health. Enjoy surfing on the feeling of fulfilment and not on misplaced consumerism.

Hunched over a latte in a café with a friend one autumn day, we were laughing about how we had lurched onto our rickety career ladders and he told me the story of how he had started out.

Freshly minted from college and stressed over the need to find work and a set of wheels to enhance his love life, he was flicking through the job pages when he spotted a medical supplies company hiring sales people.

The job looked dull, the life expectancy was on a par with First World War Fighter Pilots and he didn't have the basic skills listed. But the job would provide a car, so his ego said:

"Go for it you're a natural."

He did go for it, but luckily was unsuccessful. He reflected, realized his mistake and applied for a job that didn't supply a car, but which he was qualified for and more importantly, was interested in doing. His ego sulked for a bit and made some token "brmm brmm" noises, but soon recovered when it realized that a fulfilling job without a car stopped the waves from dumping him in a pile of seaweed at the top of the beach.

By recognizing the existence of his ego, my friend had given himself some power. The power to avoid making a stupid decision and the power to make a good decision. By choosing the right job for himself he was fulfilled. He played to his strengths and was given more responsibility, became more successful and was generally envied as a happy, healthy person.

A good decision is not necessarily one that increases our bank balance, or puts more toys in our executive playroom. It is one that increases our inner health.

E is for ego.

Think about your ego.

Picture his impish grin and sun-bleached hair. Are you using his energy to help you achieve new goals, or is he merely addicted to surfing?

How much of your behaviour can be counted as positive? How much is a prop to get you through the next week of employment terror?

Put yourself first and make positive choices that play to your strengths, increase your sense of fulfilment and boost your inner health. Think about what you are prepared to risk in order to achieve a brighter future and note that a less scary word than "risk" is *investment*.

Our ego will take a sweeping look over our double pedestal desk, with integrated penholder and monogrammed paper knife and reassure us that we are healthy.

"Honestly, you are! Look it's me, your ego talking! Now would I lie to you?"

Of course your ego would.

He's full of bullshit sometimes.

Got that? Good.

Now we can focus on the scoundrel who is causing our health to get kicked in the teeth.

Lights! Camera! Action!

It's boss time.

06

World of Bastard
Meet the villain

Here's a news flash.

Your behaviour really matters between you and your boss. It really does.

In a crisis the effects of negative behaviour can be greatly magnified. The normal pretence of civility can be dropped quicker than a hot potato and things can start turning nasty. Your inner health can hit rock bottom and then you will really start to suffer.

Time to switch on your personal radar and scan the world around you for new information.

Your boss is not there to keep you supplied with fresh coffee and chocolates, tie your shoelaces, or offer sartorial tips to help you cut a dash at the next board meeting. If you think this is his role, check to make sure you are not a fluffy, leaf chewing antelope, you dope.

Have you ever heard your beloved leader say this as a method of motivating his team:

"When I give someone a job to do I expect them to do it."

This tried and tested technique is called JDI management, or the "just do it" approach. Personally, I prefer the version that is spiked with the true emotion of the moment, called JFDI, or:

"Just fucking do it."

So, nothing about our inner health then, or worries that we may not be fulfilled, or concerns that we are on the slippery slope to becoming a Self-Fulfilling Prophecy? No of course not, and we would be naïve to think that there is any true compassion there.

And we are not naïve, we're smart.

Smart enough to understand that sometimes organizations need us and sometimes they don't. Sometimes we do it to ourselves and sometimes we are innocent drones smoked out of the beehive for reasons of space, economy, or just plain stupidity.

To ensure we keep both feet in the bubbling foot spa of reality, we need to develop some insights into our boss.

We need to understand his basic operating methods and how he responds to stressful situations, because once we understand his likely behaviour, we can plan ahead to avoid denting our inner health.

However, he is not going to be charitable and leave us alone in the stationery cupboard with a photocopier full of gleaming white paper and his personal personnel file. No way. Nor is he going to change any of his behaviour.

That would be too easy and he is far too busy doing bossy things to make our life any easier.

Instead, we could research safe cracking techniques from the local crime lord and break into the personnel office one night, but that's a bit risky. Firstly, our local Mister Big is unlikely to be listed in the telephone directory, which means having to hang around some unsavoury street corners out of office hours. And secondly, who knows what dread diseases are lurking in the personnel office?

Are all your jabs up to date?

Remember too, that your boss has the whole might of the supporting organization behind him. Sure, people go to tribunals and win thousands to make up for their injured pride and people also buy lottery tickets and win millions. These two options are very similar. They could both happen, but are both long shots and not worth building your life around.

Developing insights into people is a bit like trying to swim the Channel.

You are either a pasty looking tub of lard thrashing about in the water, or you're in the support boat with a hot chocolate. You either get stuck in and see what happens, or you sit on the sidelines and observe from a safe distance.

However, as time is likely to be against us, we are not going to swim the Channel this time. That is too far and we need to avoid sinking. Instead we'll go for a more manageable distance, which is useful without being exhausting.

The starting point is to consider your boss's general operating environment. From there we can move on to sketch out a basic model of behaviour types. Note the word "basic" again. In an emergency the basic tools are the ones that you have ready to hand and are therefore the most useful.

Nose clip on? Sick bag at the ready? Righty-ho, off we go.

Generally speaking, bosses inhabit two types of business, in the same way that bats hang upside down, either in caves, or in church towers.

The two types are family run businesses and shareholder businesses. Both may have family members in them and have shares available for purchase. However, there are several differences when it comes to understanding your boss.

For our purposes we'll define a family run business as one where the boss is part of an active family dynasty. These can be small and unobtrusive, but ignore them at your peril.

A shareholder business is one where the boss or boss's boss is genuinely answerable to a properly constituted board of directors.

In their crudest form a family run business can be little more than a benign dictatorship and often they're not that benign. Whereas, a shareholder business can be an impersonal meritocracy, with a dictatorship hiding behind it.

Both types have a habit of putting emotion before logic and in all cases it's the personality and behaviour of the top dog that sets the atmosphere and style for the whole organization. Is he a cuddly Retriever, a yappy little Westie, or a dignified but insane Red Setter?

We'll look at each type in turn and see what nuggets of gold we can pan out from the mess of business life.

Let's think about family businesses first.

A family run business that is struggling to survive will pull in its genetic horns and lop off all those people who are not blood relatives. Even if this means the remaining crew have a significantly higher than average number of fingers and a greatly reduced ability to make proper decisions.

Key decisions about people are justified on economic grounds, but are really based on who you have Sunday lunch with, not what you contribute during your working week.

Family run businesses are often ruthless to the point of brutality. For unfortunate professionals who have tangled with a Mom-and-Pop outfit on the slide, it's like being dragged naked through a thorn bush. Your plums get snagged and bruised. Ooof. Not nice.

The family members in a family run business often think of themselves as coolly detached professionals, but in reality are hopelessly caught up in the emotional turbulence generated by their drooling kinsmen. They pay scant regard for the feelings of faithful workers left out in the cold, and 20 years of loyal service can turn to ashes before your eyes. The family must come first.

So, if you have been shafted, or are in the process of being shafted, do not despair because ultimately you will leave and learn and evolve and will go on to greater successes. They will rot in their own mess because they are caught up in their own Self-Fulfilling Prophecy. Don't pity them. Life is too short.

The excuse used to remove you and send you onto the next phase of your life journey may be:

"We need to let you go because business is bad and we have to make some tough economic decisions."

The truth sitting behind it is more likely to be this:

"We need to let you go because I cannot face sacking my nitwit of a nephew, or shutting the loss making operation that my little brother struggles to manage. Next year we may be bankrupt, but we'll suck our teeth and write it off to bad luck."

Many people have fallen foul of this and it stinks.

It stinks because on joining you would have been reassured that:

"We run our business on professional lines and need people like you to help grow our profits. Who knows, perhaps one day you could have a stake it in! You may even be running it!"

No chance.

Not even after hell froze over, we had a month of Sundays and you danced with the Druids around Stonehenge under a blue moon are you going to be allowed to get so much as a fingernail on the tiller of the family business. That would rank at the same level as being allowed to sleep with the boss's wife.

In most cases your boss would rather you slept with the old trout than mess up his precious business.

On the other hand . . .

Shareholder companies tend to be a different matter.

Personnel managers are usually present in these, lurking in the dark spaces behind the trash compactor where no one goes after dark. In theory you can expect to be treated with a tiny bit more respect, although the personnel people will do their best to ensure this is a chilly experience. However, in spite of their charm bypasses, they can be counted on to comply with the law and give you a reasonably fair hearing.

The problem with a shareholder company is that you may genuinely be out of luck when the whiplash from a corporate reshuffle flays the skin from your backside.

A shareholder business, if not run on family lines, will take a broad view of its assets and its capacity to generate cash and will act accordingly by making snips and tucks to reshape itself. However, it can sometimes saw off an arm without realizing that the hand it just discarded was wearing a couple of valuable signet rings.

When it realizes its mistake, it will shrug and say:

"C'est la vie, accidents happen. Let's move on. What's next on the agenda?"

Your termination excuse is likely to be more plausible than one from a family run business, but it may not be any more truthful:

"We have to let you go because of the need to refocus our attention on core activities. Despite your valued work we cannot find a place for you within the new organizational chart."

The probable truth from the depths of the boardroom dog kennel is:

"Our managing director has distemper and is putting his latest madcap scheme into action. This cunningly involves ditching all the cash generators to ensure the board stay on their paws. This bold move is based on a pattern of tea leaves one of our Type B Consultants has been studying over the last six months and although you have a lot of skills and are a genuine asset, we do not need you for the foreseeable future. We'll miss having you around, though. For at least five minutes. Goodbye."

Although you are good at what you do, they just don't need you for now. In the great scheme of the Grand Plan, you are a tiny little plastic cog in a giant all-consuming steel reinforced wheel. If they have made a mistake they don't really care.

A corporate puppy was sent abroad for a job interview, to be measured up for an internal promotion back to the motherland. His meeting, which he had carefully rehearsed, flowed smoothly. He was tipped off unofficially that he had an excellent chance of success. Then after his boss had returned from a trip to the same overseas office, to collect the latest instalment of the grand plan, he was pulled to one side:

"I have some news for you," his boss said.

"Did I get the promotion?" the puppy asked.

"No. We're making you redundant."

"Fuck!"

"The whole of our operation is being downsized. Goodbye."

POW! Just like that. No warning. Chopped.

The puppy dusted himself off, picked the bits of shrapnel out of his drinking bowl and then used his severance package to spend the summer on holiday with his family. He soon found a new job with greatly reduced business travel and his internal health increased considerably. He became a happy puppy.

A colleague in a shareholder business relayed a conversation which occurred the day after his buddy had been downsized, made redundant, terminated, released. Take your pick of the terminology, it's all the same thing. The conversation ran something like this:

Boss

Thank you for dropping by. We need to put together a forward forecast of our capacity requirements for the plant. How do we do that?

Colleague

I have no idea and you've just removed the one person in the business who could have helped you.

Boss

Oh, bugger. Why are you not able to help then?

Colleague

Because you said that long-range planning was only for academics and I was to concentrate my efforts on fire fighting.

Boss

Did I say that? Oh dear. Well, thank you for your time and let me know if you have any ideas.

Colleague
Of course.

Two months later the boss was downsized too, in part for making a balls-up of the reorganization. After all, the undead of personnel need a constant supply of fresh meat to keep them properly nourished. If they've chomped through the management layers, then watch out you senior types. You're just a fuck-up away from becoming an hors d'oeuvre.

Whichever type of business you work in there will be a meeting before you are re-deployed into the next phase of your career. This is where the details of your impending departure, sorry, your *new challenge*, will be revealed to you.

If you're on the ball, your business antennae will have started to twitch before this. The pheromones of fate are wafting on the breeze and you will have already picked up some danger signals:

Has your boss attended any unexpected meetings?

Has he started to sound cagey about future plans?

Have people unexpectedly cancelled holidays?

Are your juniors getting lippy?

Have they started missing deadlines, or flouting the usual chain of command?

All of these things point to rumblings that could have major consequences, so notice them and be warned. Life is going to change.

When companies decide to make some changes there will be two possible outcomes for you.

Either you will be part of the in-crowd and will have to cope with the fallout from the change, or you will be part of the dead-duck brigade and will be ruthlessly hunted down. Quack. Bang.

To get the best from either outcome, it is important to anticipate both options and have a rudimentary plan of action up your sleeve. This is because you will need to:

A. Remain in control of your stress levels.
B. Stay on top of your emotions.
C. Ensure that you choose the most appropriate behaviour.

If not, you could snap and throw coffee over someone, slash their tyres, or in extreme cases torch their business. All three could end up in a nasty court case, under the hostile glare of your local press, who will run endless headlines about the time you fiddled your expenses by treating a few gin and tonics as "snacks".

An old Irish saying wisely has it thus:

"When setting out for revenge dig two graves. One for your victim and one for you."

A 30-second burst of satisfaction is nothing compared to a lifetime of regret and perhaps even a few months behind bars, sharing a cell with three hairy villains. If you're after success then the only sensible option is to maintain the professional high ground and never ever surrender it.

Aim to retain your dignity and poise because doing this when all around is a heaving mass of bad management and uncertainty is one of the most health giving actions you can take for yourself.

In medieval times, when Type B Consultants were chucked in the village stocks on sight and pelted with rotten eggs, the lord of the manor would build his spanking new castle on a hill, where he could command a decent view over the proletariat. Where would you have built your castle? In a valley? In a river? In a swamp?

Always make a dash for the high ground and fight tenaciously with your ego to stay there. Don't let the little bugger surf you into danger.

The trick in a tricky situation is to focus hard and remain focused.

Your best mate at work, who regularly brings you piping hot cappuccino, is not going to dig you out of a hole. The winking flirt in the marketing department, who lives in a haze of intoxicating French perfume, is not going to raise a single plucked eyebrow to support you in your hour of need.

You have to face facts. You don't have any friends in your organization. Not because you smell, or wear brown shoes with a charcoal suit, but because your colleagues do not want to be involved in your shit fight. Political poo is toxic, stains your shirt and leaves you a marked person.

Oh sure, you may have acquaintances, but do not be fooled. You have no idea who is talking to whom. A trusted confident can become a treacherous back stabber in the time it takes to type an e-mail. They will not risk their future to support you openly, and open support is what you need, not some kind of lame agreement for "peace in our time". To stay focused you need to concentrate on:

A. Thinking about your boss – anticipate his (or her) moves.

B. Thinking about yourself – what do you really want to happen?

C. Reacting to the unfolding situation – in healthy ways.

This is not a safe time for you or your family, when stress levels reach interstellar proportions and even the cat manages to wangle a prescription for tranquillizers. You will need to retain your dignity and prepare for the unexpected. Deep down you always knew there was no excuse for not being prepared for the unexpected.

To help maintain your laser sharp focus it is worth remembering that, in effect, your boss:

Pays your mortgage.

Stocks your fridge with food.

Puts clothes on your children's backs.

Treats the mother-in-law to a weekly bottle of sherry.

Naturally, you could lose the mother-in-law with the compulsive sherry habit, but the rest is basic stuff. Your boss may be a mean bastard, but he does pay up at the end of every month, so at least have the courtesy to take a minute to understand him and think about what he may do. Forward thinking will help you to keep your head held high.

For this to work you need information.

A light buffet of information will do just fine.

There is no time to rustle up a gargantuan feast, with eight courses and wine, that will clog your arteries and bump up the chances of a coronary.

There are two main points of interest requiring information.

First, you would be advised to check out *your boss* and start to map his behaviour when under stress. We'll consider this point in a moment.

Secondly, you would be advised to assemble *your own* Personal Survival Kit and keep it in a handy place.

Neither one of these is defeatist, or will turn you into a Self-Fulfilling Prophecy. On the contrary, they can bestow a feeling of power and serenity because you know you are prepared. Your boss doesn't know this and in his smug arrogance he will assume that you're an antelope.

But you are not an antelope, you're not a dope, you're smart.

You can avoid the added stress that comes from being a helpless victim. Even if you should have your job removed from your grasp, you will look forward to your next gig and will ride out from your castle on the hill in search of new lands to conquer, with your pennant fluttering proudly in the winds of change.

Now that both types of bastard bat (family run and shareholder) have been flushed out of the darkness, it's time to consider a simple model of the type of behaviour your boss may exhibit.

To keep things both fun and memorable we'll look to the natural world to supply some handy stereotypes for us to hang our hat on. When we need helpful tools to use in an emergency we must be able to grab them in an instant. We do not have time to draw a neat flow chart or recreate the London Underground map out of bits of string and twigs.

We are unlikely to have *Old Bodger's Almanac of Management Theory* in a pocket, or have the Essentials of Communication tattooed on a forearm.

Of course not, you only get that sort of lucky break in the movies.

Instead, we are likely to have a notebook, a pen and a super computer.

Not the swanky new palmtop with French windows 1897 and an illegal copy of Ninja Pizza Clones on it. No, think about the super computer parked between your ears, fully charged and ready to roar into action.

To find our stereotypes we need to travel far beyond the drab greyness of our office prison, out into the sunshine. Where the air-conditioned atmosphere hasn't been filtered and pumped full of everyone else's flu germs. To a place found in the more upmarket holiday brochures. So keep your passport handy.

The journey kicks off at work, where up to now it has been the usual sort of day, with too much paperwork cluttering up the paperless office, too little time to go for a flirt with the scented one in the marketing department and too many concerns about the recent spate of unusual events to concentrate on anything more complex than filing.

You are standing in the middle of the office, with desks and people scattered all around, when the temperature starts to rise.

You feel your shirt collar getting tight as little beads of sweat prick your skin.

The atmosphere begins to thicken and your mind tries hard to focus, but fails. (All very similar to the feelings you experience during your regular progress meeting with the boss.)

Your surroundings begin to distort and melt.

Pot plants turn into waving grasses or tall spindly trees with bright thorny leaves.

People and their desks boil away to nothing and the hum of the air conditioning is replaced by the whirr of buzzing insects. Vultures flap lazily, high above you in the cobalt sky. A hot, dusty breeze licks an ear lobe.

Our imagination has whisked us (club class of course, because we're on intellectual expenses here) to the hot and sultry Serengeti.

The Serengeti, home of rare and dangerous wild animals. Where exotic creatures hang out with their mates, or star in lush wildlife documentaries. Filmed against the backdrop of a shimmering sun and revealing all manner of beastly behaviour.

In these days of mega-channel mass entertainment services you can take a random pot-shot with the TV remote control at any time of the day, or night and find either a monkey playing with his coconuts, two boa constrictors in a tangle, or a pair of rhinos behind a thicket, trying to have a discreet shag.

You are now standing in the middle of this world. Your knees are trembling and sweat is pouring down your back. Your business two-piece has become a safari suit and your polished loafers are now dusty hiking boots.

You are all alone.

You have been transformed into a field researcher on a solo project and are standing in the open.

In the distance sits your 4x4 Sports Utility Hedgehog Flattener. It's parked out of sight behind a huge grey boulder and of course it's fitted with leather seats and all the toys and gizmos. If you're going to have an imaginary off-roader at least treat yourself to a top spec one.

You have a notebook in your hand, a water bottle on your hip and a pair of binoculars around your neck. A bush hat is wedged firmly on your head and although you look pretty cool, you're still on your own.

Your boss is no longer lurking in the corner office and has joined you, but not as a researcher. He has come to the party disguised as a wild animal.

Something has pushed him beyond the normal limits of pleasantries, office banter and task allocation. He is exhibiting his underlying animal tendencies and it's now a match between the two of you. You're on his home territory, isolated and beyond the reach of a rescue squad. What sort of animal is he and what pushed him into this particular corner?

What's your next move, sport?

07

The Serengeti Model
Make sense of your predicament

So here you are. Alone at last.

Unarmed and facing a potentially deadly foe. This is not good.

Once you have identified your boss and understood a bit about his likely behaviour patterns you'll be better placed to form suitable action plans to get through the crisis. Either unscathed or with the minimum of cuts, bruises and claw marks.

There are hundreds of different species of animal on the Serengeti. However, because we are producing a basic response to a crisis situation it is more practical to run with four main extremes and they are:

A. A crocodile. Snap.
B. A lion. Roar.
C. An elephant. Trumpet.
D. A meerkat. Eek.

In terms of planning and danger your boss now has one of four possibilities:

    A. He could sneak up on you and rip your leg off, like a crocodile.

    B. He could hunt you down methodically and tear your throat out, like a lion.

    C. He could panic and trample you to death, like a stampeding elephant.

    D. He could dig holes and disappear, like a meerkat.

The meerkat sounds like the best of the bunch so far, but if you trip over a burrow you could easily snap an ankle and leave yourself open to the vultures. With a nasty fracture you would be in line for a long slow death, followed by an all-you-can-eat vulture buffet lunch.

Although each species occupies its own ecological niche, they can all cause you horrific injuries, even death. This may be by design or by accident, but death is still fatal, however it is delivered.

Before taking a closer look at each type of animal it's worth pausing for a minute to recap on why you are here.

You're here because your boss has been tipped over the edge of his professional plateau. He has reverted to a basic animal stereotype in response to a stress overload in the office world.

His smooth exterior has given way to the beast that lurks just beneath the surface and his true self is revealed. Behaviour patterns are rooted largely in his subconscious and he has ducked out of his rational mature mode whilst he deals with you. His ego has launched into battle and has traded in its wetsuit and surfboard for chain mail and a war hammer.

In short, he is in animal-survival mode.

This dramatic change was brought about by an accumulation of negative experiences with you, caused by your behaviour towards him. Unknown to you, you have been stoking the fires of resentment and frustration with regular deliveries of neatly chopped wood and the water in his internal kettle has accelerated past boiling point and blown the lid off.

Sometimes the change was wrought by influences beyond your control, but a surprising amount of the time you will have contributed to the situation a good deal more than you realize.

Two forms of firewood have caused this devastating transformation and they are classified as:

A. Threat inputs.
B. Hunger inputs.

These are driving him forward to resolve the situation and he is not going to stop until one of you is waving a white flag, or is dead in a ditch.

Think of inputs as the office equivalent of poking a wild animal.

Turning up late for a meeting, or shouting with rage are the same as picking up a sharp stick and giving your animal adversary a dig in the ribs.

"Oh no!" You cry, with indignation, "If I was on the Serengeti, there's no way I would poke a lion in the ribs."

Of course you wouldn't, so why do it at work?

Your boss may be a swine and worthy of a decent poke

now and again, but it's really not going to help. When the threat inputs or the hunger inputs have reached saturation level he will be forced into action.

And right now your boss has had enough of your irritating attitude to last him a lifetime. The first step to enlightenment is to consider the two varieties of input because they are the plastic sprue of our model, which holds all the bits together.

A threat input is an action that causes your boss a degree of pain or fear.

Threat inputs can be direct, when you say it to his face, or indirect, when you tell one of his close colleagues. People are easily threatened if they feel you are smarter than they are, so openly laughing at his presentation, or loudly announcing that you've just found the obvious flaw in his new mega-strategy will not help towards the next promotion.

You can intimidate him by making it clear that you want his job. Or his office. Or a cosy tête-à-tête with his boss.

You also need to be aware of relationship chains, which are scattered everywhere.

Who is whispering into your boss's ear? Who gets under his skin?

Indirect threats can be littered right through an organization and a crocodile can easily waddle out of the water and cause an elephant to stampede. Or a lion can charge past a meerkat and send it scurrying for cover.

Threats often arise out of the way you say something.

Criticizing, disagreeing and arguing are all sure fire ways to get you noticed. An overdose will always cause a strong reaction and can turn your boss into a stereotypical wild animal over a surprisingly short period of time.

Aggression is often met with aggression and if it isn't, then the feelings inside are still those of hurt, resentment and anger. Don't overlook people who keep their aggression boiling behind narrowed eyes. Just because a crocodile doesn't hold up a dinner-gong doesn't mean that you are not being eyed up for lunch.

A successful administrator was known for being resourceful and for designing ingenious schemes to push his employer's business forward. His boss (we'll call him boss man) always told him how he welcomed change and how he looked forward to hearing the next exciting plan.

However, the truth of it was that boss man did not buy into all that dirty change talk. In reality he was far more concerned with maintaining the status quo and pursuing his own secret agenda of self advancement. Making changes and taking risks could damage his ascent of the North Face of the Corporate Eiger and he was not going to allow a mere administrator to mess up his neat ropes and belays.

People do not like to feel vulnerable and often the ones who are the greatest advocates of change are those who actually do the least. Next time your boss pushes to make some changes, take a surreptitious look in his office. When did he last alter anything, or even sweep the dust off the top of his filing cabinet?

Boss man decided to appoint a new project manager to help run the department and our hero was first in line.

He had the experience, the skills and the winning smile.

However, without realizing it he had also threatened a risk-averse colleague on a number of occasions with his desire to make progress. This colleague would complain to boss man, who would listen sympathetically and roll his eyes Heaven-ward.

When the new job was posted, the colleague lost no time in setting up a meeting with boss man to remind him about the need to choose the right candidate who would be "sympathetic" to the risk of change.

The administrator was overlooked for a deserved promotion and the spineless backstabbing colleague glided into the new post.

Outwardly, boss man looked the same as he had always done. He had not suddenly grown a fur coat or a bendy trunk, but inwardly he had responded to the threat of change by moving into a more extreme position. As a result of this, his subsequent behaviour can be viewed as being similar to that of a particular wild animal.

This reaction was predictable and could have been foreseen by the administrator. He could have tried to understand his boss's position and fears. He could have tried to sell his good ideas to him, instead of launching them at him. He could have asked his boss for some advice. He could have put together an action plan to try and deal with the problem. He could have done something positive, but he didn't.

He could also have paid closer attention to the overload of the threat inputs from his colleague, which gave the fat sneak the opportunity to pitch for the promotion.

Such emotions are the flowing rivers of office politics and can create dangerous eddies and undercurrents. The name of the game is to be alert to the other person and not to assume that you are Mr Fabulous. Sometimes you may be too dogmatic, or narrow minded, or just plain blunt. People don't like this. And if you chortle at this notion, look at your feet. Do you have hooves instead of toes?

The best way to understand the connections between the rivers and the streams coursing through your business world is to map them.

Have a go at making a list of the people in your organization that you deal with each week. Put an animal type against each person and then link him, or her, to the person whom they are most likely to talk to when they're in a backstabbing mood.

Reflect on actual conversations. When did you find yourself having to explain yourself to your boss? How did he know there was a problem? What was the incentive for the sneak to contact him in the first place?

Organizational politics can be a minefield, so a top tip to avoid over complexity is to focus on the people who you feel could do the most to undermine your position with your boss. Work hard at understanding your core relationship (the one between you and your immediate boss) and maintain a watching brief on the others.

The second type of input is hunger.

Hunger is an absence.

You are often the source of that absence. Absence can be physical or mental. It can include switching off in a meeting, office daydreaming, or not listening to his scintillating strategy presentation. Yawn, yawn.

You can turn up late for work, or not turn up at all. You can throw a sickie. You can be late for meetings, or you can overlook the deadline for a piece of work. You can forget to reply to an e-mail, or not make that important telephone call, which may have clinched the sale of the century.

All of these will annoy your boss. Funny that.

All of them add up after a time and your boss may be a bastard, but he has a good memory. And if he doesn't, then there are always the secret police in the personnel department to whisper into his ear.

A supervisor would laugh during a meeting when asked for her monthly report.

"Um, I forgot it", she would giggle. Or,

"I didn't have enough time to complete it."

The reply to this childish excuse was always:

"But you've had all month and I only asked for a single sheet of A4!"

One day the comedienne even offered the following excuse:

"The dog ate it."

And she didn't even own a dog. Only a couple of moth-eaten cats, who couldn't have digested a whole sheet of paper. A small corner possibly, but not a whole sheet. The supervisor never switched on to the fact that her boss needed the report to take to a meeting with the senior management and its absence was a severe embarrassment to him.

She never realized that saying "the dog ate it" was an obvious code for "I couldn't care less for you or your rotten business."

Unfortunately, her boss had cracked the code and eventually the lady in question was pulled to one side and politely told that her services were no longer required.

"Why?" she said, shocked. "Why me? What have I ever done?"

A good rule of thumb is that an accumulation of threat inputs usually proves fatal, whereas the outcome from a fist full of hunger inputs is likely to be a severe mauling.

Remember though, that you may still succumb to your wounds.

Cue the vultures.

It's tough on the Serengeti.

> **!** **●** Think about how you annoy your boss. What have you done to make him feel unsafe recently? What things have you not completed on time, or failed to deliver at all? Be honest here. When did you boast to a colleague about your lack of action or about shouting your mouth off in a meeting? When you have some things, turn to the back of the book and complete Threat & Hunger Inputs (page 203).

So, after many years of loyal and devoted service to your benign and thoughtful boss you are standing on the dusty African plains. Armed with your wits and a water bottle and facing a wild animal. But how do you know which wild animal you are facing?

The basic behaviour of a cornered, or annoyed, or frightened creature is straightforward. As we are travelling light we only need to remember four extreme types to serve us in times of crisis. So therefore, to determine what sort of an animal your boss is there are only two questions to ask:

A. Is he stable?

B. Is he confrontational?

Look through your binoculars at him.

What do you see?

Flick back a couple of pages in your researcher's notepad. What happened yesterday? What behaviour did you see for yourself, or hear about back at base camp?

Does your boss have a three-foot long jaw, crammed with two-inch teeth and rows of scaly green spines on his back?

Well then he's a crocodile. Easy.

As it's not likely to be that obvious, we will now shuffle through some clues to help pin down the animal in front of us.

Stable people like to plan and think and plan a bit more. They may appear as "cold" types.

Unstable people are more spontaneous and emotional. They may appear as "hot" types. They may well spew out ideas on the spur of the moment, each one landing on top of the previous one, like a volcano spitting out lumps of lava. They may be good ideas, but you are unlikely to have much time to think about them before the next one hits you.

A stable person might say that they were disappointed with you, whereas an unstable person might shout at you across the room, or call you a complete failure.

A stable person would sit calmly explaining why your pay rise this year was the size of a whelk's fart, whereas an unstable person would shuffle in their seat, wring their hands, and drivel on about the economy and the fact that it wasn't their decision anyway.

Stable people put business tasks before team feelings, whereas unstable people use weasel words to try and make you feel better.

So, ask yourself the first question: *Is your boss stable or unstable?*

Here is the second question again: *Is your boss confrontational?*

A person who is confrontational will often block your path and thrust their jaw close to your face, with a no-fear approach. They will talk to you before you have a chance to sit down, or they will invade your comfort zone and sit next to you.

They will announce an impeding visit with a fanfare of trumpets. On arrival they will crush your hand, stand on your toes, look you in the eye and say:

"What the hell is that mess over there?"

They ask direct questions, like to give orders and they love giving you unwanted advice.

A non-confrontational person will tend to shy away from contact, or will surprise you. They can appear nervous if they are unstable types, as the emotion leaks out through their fingertips. Or if they are stable types they may appear to be sneaky. This bunch tend not to use their eyes to smile. They let their mouths do all the work in a cold, gruesome way.

Non-confrontational people often feel a need to hide behind something in a meeting, such as a computer screen or a pile of paper. Watch them build a tiny wall when they see you heading in their direction and note their body language. Their posture may become more hunched than with confrontational people, or they may sit with their legs twisted to one side, pointing away from you. They will usually have trouble maintaining eye contact.

Non-confrontational types will write to you, instead of telephoning, to express their frustration at an incident, or after an event which annoyed them. Your response will be:

"Well you could have bloody told me yesterday, when I was standing right next to you!"

A really non-confrontational person may not even tell you that there is a problem and will just seethe inwardly. You may mistake their silence for agreement, or worse, assume that they didn't notice the problem. They did. They are always alert.

Never make the mistake of writing off a non-confrontational boss as "weak" or "toothless", because they can have a heart of wrought iron and they will sort you out in the end.

So, ask yourself the second question: Is your boss confrontational? Yes or no?

Having swept through the two basic questions we can apply them to a straightforward matrix to sift the animal inside the boss. What sort of animal is dominating your life? The answer is below:

If you are having trouble deciding which quadrant your boss fits into, then fret not. The important thing is to decide how he behaves towards *you* most of the time. You can ask yourself: How do I feel when I see him or speak to him unexpectedly?

For example, when the phone rings and he makes you jump out of your skin, or you bump into him in the corridor and he bares his teeth at you.

The Serengeti Boss Type Model (SBTM)

	Crocodile Snap	**Lion** Roar
Stable		
Unstable	**Meerkat** Eek	**Elephant** Trumpet
	Non-Confrontational	**Confrontational**

There may even be a few bosses out there who sit in the exact centre of the model, with sensible, friendly, balanced behaviour. We don't care about these because:

A. They are too few in number to worry about; and

B. If you work for one of these you probably haven't purchased this book anyway.

For now, choose the animal type which you see or sense most of the time in most situations, particularly when they are stressed. Stress almost always takes him back to a default position, where despite his designer suit, polished brogues and chunky porn star bracelet he will have reverted to his basic underlying animal type. You can always change your choice later on, if you need to.

Now, although we may have chosen an animal type, it's still worthwhile to cross reference our initial assumptions with the results of a bit of quick and dirty secondary evidence gathering activity. We are researchers, after all, so let's do some research and make some notes.

Fortunately, we are not going to need a lock of hair because DNA testing is restricted to sci-fi movies, the police and the upper echelons of the personnel research scientists experimenting down in the dungeons.

Instead we will stick with things we can easily identify and leave all the technical stuff to those people with a plank between their eyebrows and their hairline.

A big clue comes from the way our boss shakes hands.

This is a cheap, non-invasive diagnostic technique which is easily overlooked.

Number one: The Sniffer. A crocodile will shake your hand reluctantly, but firmly and will sniff the air near to you to sense what you're thinking.

Number two: The Crusher. A lion will clamp your hand in a steel grip and will unnerve you by standing a little too close to make it clear that you're being sized up. He will then pump your arm vigorously, as if testing to see just how firmly it's attached to the rest of you.

Number three: The Wobbler. An elephant will shake your hand with a sort of childish enthusiasm, using a softish grip and plenty of wrist movement. He focuses on the action of hand shaking, without noticing if you are the floor sweeper, or the chairman of the board.

Number four: The Stroke. A meerkat will hate this sort of thing and may prefer to wave meekly at you, or keep his paws stuffed in his pockets. If you keep your arm outstretched he will eventually offer a paw and you will enjoy the sensation of having your hand being nervously stroked by a piece of wet lettuce. Your hand may now feel damp and your surprise may draw a nervous apology from the trembling creature.

Sometimes etiquette, or timing means that we lose the opportunity to shake hands at the start of the introduction. If this happens there is nothing to stop you from being assertive and greet them for a second time. Stick out your arm and see what happens:

"Hello Mr Big Boss, we forgot to shake hands (extend arm). How are you today?"

Handshakes may not be available in a crisis situation, so instead try focusing on one defining aspect of behaviour to identify the beast that stands before you:

A crocodile is *cunning*.

A lion likes to *leap*.

An elephant may have *emotional* outbursts.

A meerkat may be *missing*.

This is the basic double check to make sure you have identified the right species and if time is against you use these filters to see what sort of animal is in front of you.

❗ Go on, think about him (or her) again and choose an animal type. Then
⬤ turn to your Personal Survival Kit and complete The Serengeti Boss Type Model (page 204). Circle one animal. Use a pencil if you're not sure.

Pause for a moment and remember where you are.

You have left the "safe" confines of your office environment for the unfamiliar and dangerous Serengeti.

You have a 4x4 parked out of reach and a wild animal is in front of you.

You look cool wearing your designer Safari gear. We'll ignore the sweat patches.

With a water bottle on your hip and a notebook in your hand the aim is to collect some more useful information, which is where we're heading next.

And, if you can only see a fuzzy blob in the haze and have not worked out what sort of beast it is yet, do not despair. Read on and reflect.

08

Field Research
Gather insight and information

The Serengeti model is there to help us understand the sort of threat we are facing. Does our boss exhibit confrontational behaviour? And is he stable? These are the two key questions that form the basis of the model.

However, for some bosses you may be chewing the end of your pencil and squinting into the distance. Their animal type may require some more information in order to pin them down.

Unfortunately this information is not carved into a handy acacia tree, or daubed on a bit of rock. As field researchers we need to use our eyes and ears to pick up the clues which will fill our notebook with useful scribbles.

Then once we have written up our notes, the insights will help to focus our minds on possible options for action.

A sneaky way to diagnose the animal type is to use third party information.

Be a bit careful though, as you may be basing your decision on hearsay and not evidence. Some hearsay may contain a few grains of truth, so there's no need to ignore it totally. Simply treat it with respect and don't make any life changing decisions based on it in isolation.

However, using third party information can be a useful exercise if you are new in an organization, or your boss is based at head office and is not available for easy inspection.

The lazy way to gain an insight into your new boss is to ask around and see what sort of a response you get. Ask open questions that elicit behavioural styles. Some examples are given below. Have fun by inventing your own.

What is he like doing an appraisal?

A *crocodile* may say: "You need to work on those development points." Don't wait for the praise, as there's none on the way.

A *lion* may say: "You've done some good things and some bad things. Let me tell you about the bad things". He doesn't care about the good things, as they fall under the heading of "just doing your job".

An *elephant* may say: "You may not agree with this, but it's what I think." Unfounded criticisms that are based on last week's activity and ignore the contribution you made six months ago. Emotion before reason is at work here.

A *meerkat* may say: "I'm er, nearly finished, so um, let's make a start and we can, er fill in the detail as we go." His opinions are your opinions. Easy, but you are never going to develop much.

How does he communicate your objectives to you?

A crocodile may give you a chilly electronic briefing: "Let's discuss your objectives for the next quarter. I'll e-mail them to you." The message contains enough objectives to keep you out of his way for the next 20 years.

Lions like the chance to demonstrate their supremacy to your face: "We need to set some objectives." He hands you a sheet of paper. "Do you have any questions?" You wouldn't dare poke him by asking.

An elephant will tend to bluster: "I need to give you some objectives. Um, here's the first three. I don't agree with all this 'objectives' nonsense." That's encouraging. After all, defining the priorities is a key part of his job.

Meerkats can just be useless: "Right then, let's talk about it. What would you like to do for the next quarter?" You assemble a list, but are suspicious that it may not be in line with the overall corporate direction. This could backfire on you in the future when the meerkat disappears in a crisis and drops you in the shit.

How do people tend to describe him?

Crocodiles can be: cold, thoughtful, tough, decisive, stubborn and organized. Either you never see him, or he turns up unexpectedly when there is a problem which you didn't know he knew about.

Lions can be: scary, intimidating, clever, successful and visionary. You know when he's cross and if he wants your opinion he'll tell you what it is.

Elephants can be: friendly, helpful, noisy, unpredictable, spiteful and vindictive. Nice people on the surface, but watch out for sudden mood swings and their big fat feet.

Meerkats can be: quiet, shy, nervous, disorganised, forgetful and sweaty. Either his office door is bolted shut, or he ambles round the office and wastes everyone's time with his nervous chit chat, whilst constantly checking to make sure his escape route is clear.

What is he like in a meeting?

A crocodile will often use guile and cunning to achieve their desired outcome: He has a very strong sense of what he wants and gets grumpy very easily if others prolong the discussion. He hates being challenged. A croc likes to be the power behind the "leader" and will do anything to retain his position of control. You may be the nominated chairman, but that's just detail and of no consequence to him. Favourite tactics include skipping agenda points, or pulling out files that you didn't expect and firing questions at you. He will have *already* taken soundings from all the delegates prior to the meeting and will play these out as the meeting progresses to suit his own agenda. The meeting is there to rubber stamp his plan and if things go against him he will end the session, slip back into the water and paddle away.

In short, a crocodile will manipulate people so the group consensus fits his perception of the world, which is the only one that matters to him.

A lion will look forward to all meetings and will spend some time sharpening his claws beforehand: He will often have a brisk manner about him to keep the antelope moving about, so they tire quickly. He loves being in charge, and unlike a crocodile he makes it clear that he's the top cat. Often quick to disagree and express his own opinions, he may even start a fight just so he can savage someone for sport. Lions also have a habit of giving people intense looks to unnerve them and they like to talk about "biting off the problem" or "chewing it over".

A lion will sometimes idly pick his teeth with a blade of grass and then suddenly leap in with fresh ideas. He will aim to achieve an outcome that matches his preferred solution, which may be the one he's just thought of. Sudden leaps, although predictable behaviour, still tend to surprise people, who had wrongly assumed the lion was daydreaming. Consensus is not in his vocabulary and if he was daydreaming, it was probably about fresh meat.

The dear old elephant may be lampooned as a duffer by their colleagues whilst assembling for the meeting: He will tend to kick off as a friendly and thoughtful leader, trying to include everyone and ensuring an even-handed discussion. Then he can lose sight of the meeting's objective and let people chat on, even if they are not really contributing. Often these diversions soak up loads of meeting time, but at least all the participants get to discuss their favourite soap opera and find out just which supposedly dead character has reappeared, having spent the last ten years secretly living in a shed at the bottom of the garden.

Elephants, being moody lumps, will tolerate this drivel for so long and then having realized they have wasted most of the afternoon, will switch from pleasure to irritation and try to get the meeting back on track. Sometimes they even succeed. The results of the meeting can be frustratingly small for everybody and in the last few minutes a bored lion may nip the ankles of the big grey beast and attempt to get people to commit to actually doing stuff.

However, if the meeting calls for emergency action the elephant is likely to be stirred into an immediate and thoughtless response. He will panic, overlook the core objective and then force the team to pursue a single goal that may be inappropriate. He will trample the rest of the group in a personal stampede to achieve a result. Any result.

A meerkat leading a meeting is a bit unlikely: He will only be really comfortable in the observer role, where he can watch the meeting unfold from the sidelines. Quick to dump work on you and slow to interfere, the meerkat will let the meeting look after itself and will tend to sit quietly whilst the lions battle it out for supremacy. Meerkats struggle to exert any sort of authority over a group and may be seen mopping their brow with nervous fatigue. When things get out of control, the meerkat will either explode in a fit of squeaking, which everyone ignores, or will sit tight until the storm has passed, his little heart pounding with fear.

Meerkats tend to keep their opinions to themselves, or present them in such a way as to make it easy for others to overlook them. Their meetings usually end up generating a long list of vague and irrelevant actions, as they do not wish to overlook proposals coming from more confrontational characters. A good way to spot a meerkat in a meeting is by their absence of contribution and by the fact that a junior lion is likely to be occupying the leadership void they have created.

These searching questions should have helped to pinpoint some simple behavioural traits. However, if you are still struggling to define your boss, or are simply enjoying the process of identification, try to think of extreme situations.

How did he react when that crucial order failed to ship?

How did he conduct the meeting to resolve an expensive customer complaint?

How much involvement was there before he decided on the new office layout?

If your boss exhibits a range of confusing animal traits and is difficult to pin down then he may be quite self-aware and have a broad repertoire of behavioural actions. Or he may have recently had a bump on the head and simply be suffering from concussion. In both cases the best way to approach him is to focus on the animal which he appears as most often. This is probably his true self, bubbling to the surface.

Having isolated your boss's gene pool (which can be remarkably shallow) we can take a peak at a broader picture of his animal type. This can help us to think about how his subconscious is pulling the strings. He is after all a prisoner of his own inbreeding and evolutionary trajectory. Had he known this, Darwin would have had to publish a second book, called "On the Nature and Selection of Stupid, Cretinous, Pain in the Derrière Bosses".

He would have had to use Derrière, as Ass would not have sneaked past the censors.

The **crocodile** is generally the big bad guy of the bunch.

Crocodiles have been around for about 80 million years. They are clever, strong and resourceful and can survive a long time between meals. And all that time spent watching other animals evolve has allowed them to build up a fantastic amount of general knowledge, so never go one-on-one with a crocodile in a quiz. He'll beat you hands down.

Usually, they are solitary creatures, but they can work together to sort out a big problem. When wildebeest try to play the safety in numbers game the crocodiles all line up and turn into living barbed wire. Safety in numbers is all very well until you become the quadruped with a crocodile for an ankle bracelet.

Stable, calculating, planning machines, crocodiles like to think first, think second and only attack third. A crocodile will sit in his office quietly scheming. He will always have a plan and will not share it with you, unless you specifically demand to see it, or he needs your contribution to make it successful.

They are not confrontational so their behaviour can be easily overlooked. People might say "I didn't see him coming", but you could have if you looked closely enough. Crocodiles are always after someone, so the sensible thing is to assume that it's you.

If you're feeling brave then a crocodile can be safely approached when he is feeling sleepy between hearty meals. Conversely, if you stay well clear of him he may not notice you in the background and forget you are there. In an office run by a crocodile there may be a hard core of "subservient quiet types" who have merged with the wallpaper and seem to last for years.

Crocodiles are savage, effective, powerful beasts. They like to win and they do not have much thought for your feelings or welfare. To them, life is a carefully calculated plan and you are either in or out. They have an unshakeable belief that their plan is right and they do not take kindly to criticism.

As they are non-confrontational, a favourite tactic is to get another animal, such as a tame elephant, to do their dirty work. The crocodile will have taken the decision, but will often try to manipulate someone else to tackle tricky personnel issues on their behalf.

Lithe in the water, a crocodile can also outpace a human on dry land. Most of the time, they conceal their bulk in the murky soup of a handy watering hole, leaving just their nose and eyes above the surface. You have no idea what they're thinking, or when they may attack next and when they do snap at you the shock of it can be devastating.

If you have to confront a crocodile then arrange a meeting on high ground, where you can keep an eye on his arsenal.

If your boss is a crocodile he is not likely to sit in front of you and list his grievances with you, or hold a debate to decide on a course of action. He will write to you to let you know that he would like a meeting. If this is unexpected and hastily arranged, then watch out. If the crocodile is usually impossible to pin down, but suddenly has an hour free tomorrow morning your time is up.

How does he know the meeting will only take an hour?

Why has he not asked any colleagues to attend?

Why so urgent?

This is because he has all the questions and all the answers to hand. All he wants from you is to put up as little resistance as possible to avoid chipping any teeth during his attack. You should go through your Personal Survival Kit very carefully and make sure it is up-to-date and accurate.

You are going to need it.

Crocodiles are non-confrontational, cunning and deadly.

A female sales executive was driving along a sun-dappled motorway to see a couple of friendly customers when a call came through on her mobile. It was her croc-boss, a female of the species. Think of a croc with bright red lipstick and a bad perm and you get the picture.

"Was she available for a quick meeting today?"

"No. She was on the other side of the country."

"What about tomorrow? She'd only need an hour with her."

Hmmm. This was the first time in two years her croc-boss had urgently requested a meeting with no apparent agenda or preparation needed.

During the meeting, her boss, being a non-confrontational crocodile, tried to tell the saleswoman that she was being made redundant, without actually using the word "redundant". She rambled round the edges of the issue and couched the coup de grâce in bland management speak. At the end of the hour her boss drew things to a close and left the room. Afterwards, the executive pondered on her boss's comments. She sighed deeply and her heaving bosom rippled and swayed inside her designer jacket, as she tried to work out just what the hell had been said.

It was only when the poor dear attempted to stand up that she realized both of her legs had just been chewed off. And the croc hadn't even marked her expensive snakeskin shoes. Even crocs have their limits.

Unlike crocodiles, **lions** are more up front with their aggression. They have power and presence and carry an ugly set of steak knives with them, which they use to intimidate people.

Lions like to think of themselves as management royalty. They enjoy keeping their subjects in their place and they don't like being interrupted, or contradicted. They also don't tend to carry loose change, so be wary of them when approaching the coffee machine.

They mean business and may even bully weaker lions to assert their dominance and prevent challenges to the head of state.

Aggressive lions can be super-confrontational and work overtime to ensure all the other animals know they are there by pacing about their territory and looking under rocks and stones. In an office, a lion-boss would think nothing of rifling through the work on your desk, or double checking your progress with a junior colleague. It all belongs to them anyway, it just happens to be on *your* desk. They won't mind if you catch them at it, as they know it's their regal right to do as they please, when they please.

They are tactical animals, who will size you up from a distance and then saunter in, before trying to run you down. They may even indulge in a spot of practising to make sure they have the measure of you. Be patient and observant and you can spot a lion creeping about in the long grass.

This can give you time to run away. You may even be able to make it back to your 4x4 if you have enough of a head start. As they are excellent sprinters you need to know which way you will run, make sure you have your car keys to hand and check both shoelaces are tied tight. Like the crocodile, if a lion has you on his lunch menu then it's a fair chance that you will be eaten.

Preparation is the key here and when you have to get out you need to get out fast, with no time for dithering.

Lions often have a certain smugness about them that says "One day I'll get you".

If a lion-boss thinks you are competing with him then watch out, he'll stalk you night and day to prove that he's better. If the lion is a colleague and not your direct boss, then you can bet he is mauling your back. You can help yourself here by installing wing mirrors on your desk.

Predictable hunting platforms, lions have retained their carnivorous niche at the top of the food chain. You'll know when you are working for a lion when he boasts about previous successes, or the fact that he is "firm, but fair". That's just code for "firm, but aggressive really".

Start planning your escape route, today.

However, the self-appointed king of beasts tends to attack the more obvious game first and you can avoid an early mauling by staying upwind of the sick and the lame. You will still need to be alert to sudden changes in the wind direction in case the lion alters his angle of attack. Plenty of antelope have been scoffed whilst laughing and pointing at their "stupid" colleagues.

Most lions are arrogant and have a thick lazy streak running through them. This is because certain tasks are beneath their majestic magnificence. In an office managed by a lion, it is also possible to avoid attack by helpfully doing all the menial jobs.

These are usually defined as those the lion does not want to undertake himself and include making the coffee, filling the photocopier and collecting the post. Royalty does not like to get its hands dirty, old chap.

A friend of mine cut his management teeth in a small warehousing business run by a lion and an elephant. The lion would scare the shit out of everyone on a daily basis.

A standard telephone conversation about stock levels would often end with the words:

"Right, that's it, I've had enough! I'm coming over the road to sort it out myself!"

As the lion strode down the driveway, tossing his mane in the sun, all the antelope would bound out of the way, looking for cover. If they had been issued with tin hats, they would have put them on and tightened the chinstraps. No one would catch the lion's eye. The elephant would stand to one side, idly munching her way through a bale of hay.

My friend told me that he would wait in the middle of the warehouse, shivering and trying not to look too much like the dish of the day. The lion would roar up and administer an on-the-spot quiz about arcane and obscure items, which were rarely checked or dispatched. After each answer, the lion would drag my friend round the shelving to see if his answer was right. It never was (it was never going to be) and the lion exacted his revenge by verbally roughing him up about how useless he was. The elephant would remain standing to one side, oblivious to the commotion.

When he joined the company there were three managers, including him, but one of them soon left without a job to go to, having been scared to death by the lion's aggressive bullying behaviour. Eventually, one Friday afternoon the lion surprised my friend, who said that he literally jumped two inches off the floor with fear. The lion put him on the lunch menu and a week later he was finally mauled to a bloody pulp and left for the vultures. Then the lion moved on to his final victim.

Fortunately, the third manager escaped just in time and was last heard living happily in a new job, miles away from the lion.

Elephants are bulky herbivores who fritter away their days discussing the plots of soap operas and eating greenery.

However, despite their docile and slightly inept appearance, they can trample you to death, or spear you on the end of a deadly tusk. The good news to this is that if they start their run up early enough you may well have a chance to skip out of the way.

A boss does not have to be physically large to be an elephant and the pygmy sized ones are just as deadly.

They all have excellent memories, which they use to bear grudges with. They have a particular facility for logging those people who irritate them and then, being unpredictable, they may well turn on them without warning.

The best way to avoid an elephant is not to get too close to their feet or their tusks. And don't make sharp noises or throw things at them, because sudden gestures will set them off. The same applies to sudden smells, which can easily spook them.

Elephants tend to be very protective towards their "family" and will attack much more readily if these people are threatened. When you work for an elephant you can increase your chances of survival by paying close attention to the elephant's closest relationships and by sucking up to his "family".

Whilst an elephant chomps his way round the plants in your office, you can be lulled into a false sense of security and let him wander out of sight.

This can be fatal.

When he breaks cover and rushes away from danger he will flatten you by mistake.

Learn to check on his current location, which may not be easy in a business environment, so make good use of your binoculars. If you think the threat is minimal you can get in quite close, but be careful. Is that a lion sneaking up over there? Or is the elephant about to get his trunk tweaked by a crocodile? Both of these could result in an unexpected stampede.

The best way to avoid getting trampled is to ensure someone is standing between you and the elephant. A simple strategy. Heartless, but effective.

An office run by an elephant can be a fun place to be, because Old Big Ears will sit quietly getting on with his work. However, when a crisis hits, the reaction can be extreme and full of emotion. The elephant will make snap decisions and can cause people's stress levels to soar with the volume of tasks that suddenly flow their way.

The elephant will eventually calm down and survey the wreckage, but some of his big clumsy footprints will have left holes in the floor and a pile of squashed toes.

The best tactic to deploy, when facing an elephant in full flow, is to remain still. Blend in with the shrubbery and avoid catching his eye. Then tiptoe out of the way, without leaving any fearful odours behind.

A marketing assistant worked for an elephant, who was a decent-ish boss until he actually had to do some work. Usually, whilst sitting in his office drawing patterns on his whiteboard, or eating bags of salad, the elephant was harmless enough. However, when the managing director gave him a task to undertake, the elephant would soil his swivel chair and charge out of the office trumpeting like a maniac.

Panicking with the need to do something, the elephant would stride up to a member of his team, with his big ears flapping wildly and after a couple of minutes of trampling, all that would be left was a foot print in the carpet and some fibres of suit-like material. In this fashion he managed to squash four marketing assistants in three years. The remaining assistants were sad to see them go. They were also grateful they had escaped a flattening.

However, their problem was that they failed to realize the laws of probability meant playing Russian roulette with half a ton of grey imbecile was never going to give them a safe ride to retirement.

Meerkats are, on the face of it, the least threatening of the four animal types. They don't weigh a couple of tons, maul people for sport or twist your leg off. Don't be fooled though, Meerkats can still cause you serious problems.

A meerkat is cute little fellow who snacks on grubs and insects and other tasty morsels from the Serengeti snack bar. They are not known for their giant jaws, or throat tearing, or bulky weight, but they do like to dig holes. A meerkat will happily munch all day, until one of the scouts in their group spots a threat and then they high tail it down a burrow, or run about trying to avoid the eagle swooping in out of nowhere.

And the little sods just love to dig.

A meerkat-boss can open up a hole beneath you, where before there was solid ground. Or the little twitchy-nosed bastard can just vanish, when you most need him.

Both of these can be fatal.

If you trip over a burrow and break a leg you may be unable to make it back to your 4x4. You will wither and die whilst the vultures come flapping in to land and set up their picnic tables and gas powered barbecues.

Alternatively, the meerkat may be scurrying out of the way of a marauding lion, who then takes a shine to you instead.

The best way to avoid trouble is to keep looking down to see what is happening under your nose. Then look up and take note of any approaching animals.

Meerkats love company and may well congregate with other meerkats, to feel safe. A meerkat-boss may treat his office as a burrow to hide in, or may spend time chatting with you, perhaps looking for you to take a decision. He may even be seeking reassurance that the big decision he has just taken (reluctantly) really was a smart move.

They are nervous little critters on a hair trigger. They hate having to square up to people, but with the support of a group of colleagues, or by irritating a lion into action meerkats can still make their presence felt. For example, the meerkat will chat away to the lion, telling him all about your rubbish performance and eventually the royal predator will get fed up and ambush you by the coat rack.

Meerkats reach positions of boss-dom largely as a pawn in someone else's political game, or through over promotion. They can also arrive in the corner office as a result of a cock-up by personnel, who didn't realize the answers on their psychometric test were based on "my favourite hobbies" and not on reality.

An office run by a meerkat is probably being run by a crocodile, a lion or an elephant who step in to the void left when the meerkat disappears down his burrow. The meerkat will preen, assume he is good at delegating and that he has things in apple pie order, but the truth is he has abdicated his management responsibility.

There is often tension between the meerkat and the assumed boss.

Choose a side and stick with it.

You may be able to convince the meerkat to get rid of the assumed boss, or you may be able to build a power base and become largely untouchable. However the whole set up may eventually be swept away by a more senior boss, fed up with the squabbling.

A group of meerkats built up a successful consultancy business. Their innovative solutions sold themselves and the customers rolled in. When the business took a tumble, after a key client went west, they knew instinctively what to do.

Downsize?

Get a loan to make up for the lack of cash?

Go out selling?

No, of course not, that would be too easy.

What they did instead was to sit around in their board room, drink whisky and twitch anxiously. Every day for two weeks they would set up the bar at 9.00 am sharp, crack open a bottle of Serengeti Single Malt and drink and wait for the telephone to ring. It never did.

Four weeks later their staff arrived for work one day to find the doors locked and a note pasted up announcing that the business had gone bust. The meerkats blamed it on the recession and said there were no steps they could have taken to prevent it.

The meerkats were nowhere to be found. They had tunnelled out through the back of the building and were long gone.

There may be a few days each millennium when your boss will not readily exhibit obvious stereotypical behaviour.

If the situation is not sufficiently extreme you can be fooled into thinking that you are still working with another human being, who cares for your emotional health and well being.

Be careful, because the animal always lurks close to the surface.

> **!** **●** After all that research it will help your chances of survival to note down some of the characteristics your boss exhibits when he is in his animal position. This will help you to remain in awareness and avoid getting a nasty surprise. Think about what he does when stressed, or how he gets his own way? For example, crocodiles may plan quietly, lions may start giving you evil looks, elephants may have little outpourings of emotion and meerkats may hide. Look again at the sections which relate to the animal type your boss has been identified with. Then turn to your Personal Survival Kit and jot down a few helpful pointers. Complete Field Research (page 205).

Lastly, as we identified before, there is a final group of bosses, who when stressed, manage to maintain an even balance between confrontation and stability.

These people, rare as rocking horse shit, remain in the exact middle of the four squares. They sit on the centre cross and behave in a straightforward adult manner.

You don't feel that you are being eaten for lunch, tripped over, or trampled to dust.

You may not like what you hear, you may not agree with it, but you will understand it and will not have the feelings of rage, frustration or injustice that you get by dealing with a crocodile, a lion, an elephant or a meerkat.

These bosses are largely unknown to modern science. If you find one, have him stuffed and mounted for posterity.

At the end of our field research, we need to take a look at our notebook, to see what we have learned.

To begin with, the most important working relationship you have is the one between you and your boss.

He is not your friend. If he says he is, he's lying.

Bosses exist in family run businesses, where they can act in unfair ways, or they can exist in shareholder companies, where they can act in unexpected ways.

They are irritated by inputs, which they perceive as a threat or as hunger.

These inputs are the same as poking a wild animal with a sharp stick.

All the little jabs leave a mark and add up over time. Inputs can come from colleagues or your boss's boss, so you need to be aware of relationship chains and where you sit within them.

When the inputs reach a critical level your boss will get pushed over the edge and will revert to an animal state until the situation has been resolved. Your boss's behaviour will be driven by his subconscious, which can be categorized by referring to one of the four extreme animal stereotypes.

The office will melt away and you will find yourself standing on the Serengeti, facing danger and uncertainty.

In front of you there could be:

- A cunning crocodile.
- A leaping lion.
- An emotional elephant.
- A missing meerkat.

Your first aim is to keep out of danger.

If this fails, the second one is to anticipate the attack and give yourself enough of a head start to make it to your 4x4 and to safety.

And above all else:

Make sure you know which animal you are facing and try not to antagonize it.

09

Time to Plan
Get a wiggle on and think

Knowing something about behaviour and understanding that the world is full of wild animals can reduce your stress levels.

However, to ensure that your inner health is maintained you will have to take some positive steps for yourself.

You will actually have to do something about it and plan for the immediate future.

Since the industrial revolution in the eighteenth century, people have been griping about poor conditions, poor pay and the ever-present danger of losing an appendage from an unguarded piece of machinery. In the twenty-first century, despite all the legislation to improve conditions, people are still griping.

At a smart party for middle management types a disgruntled gentleman spouted off about the lack of loyalty in business today, but nobody listened. They already knew the central business truth that rapid evolution and long-term loyalty to staff are not bedfellows.

If the average tenure in a job tends to be between two and five years these days, then you will probably have between nine and twenty-two jobs between starting your career and starting your retirement. That's nine to twenty-two different roles between the ages of 21 and 65. The chances of meeting a few bastards along the way are high.

If you don't plan for the future these job changes are going to come as a surprise to you. You may even blunder around and moan about the lack of loyalty.

Loyalty? Who are you kidding?

The only person who is truly loyal to you is *you*.

And perhaps, your immediate family.

No employer cares two hoots about you when the going gets tough, because you then become part of the baggage train that is slowing down the whole convoy.

So, wise up, give yourself some options, get a plan and think about the actions you can take.

In the dusty past a successful business came under pressure from an aggressive foreign competitor. They had to make radical changes to stay in the game. Most of the workforce was under threat of redundancy, or redeployment to another site.

During a lunch break, one rainy day, the managers were chatting in the canteen. Their impromptu consensus was that Old Ginger Wig easily scooped the award of *Manager most likely to be first out the door*. This dubious accolade was based largely on the fact that Rug Man could not work a computer, had no obvious management skill and was (most damningly) old. However, the rather biased judging panel failed to consider his excellent trade skills.

Smart companies rarely get rid of key productive skills first. No matter how heavily manned you are on the oars, your corporate Roman galley will not slow down if your first action is to throw some ballast overboard. And ballast means *management*.

Sadly, most managers fail to grasp this and are surprised when they are thrown to the sharks before anyone else. They take it as a personal insult, instead of a practical business strategy to save costs in the least risky way.

When a top-to-bottom clear out is necessary, companies tend to start at the top of the pyramid and work downwards, so managers need to be more concerned than the good people of the production, or service departments. These people help the company to earn money, whereas most of the people above them spend it.

Back to the canteen.

On that particular day I was with the group of managers chatting about the possible changes, although I had not voted for Old Ginger Wig. Instead, I had voted for myself.

I surprised everyone by suggesting that they should worry less about picking on the wig wearer and more about preparing their own Personal Survival Kits.

They were amazed. I was amazed at their amazement.

They reminded me that I was safe, so why should I bother with one? After all, had I not recently been booked onto an expensive training course? Was I not the one with the promising "Executive" future?

I reminded them that you cannot un-spend money, so who cares if you have some training left to complete? If the boat is taking on water today then you have no future and training is the least of your worries.

After some prompting, they agreed that if they were, for example, going to fly a snarling fighter-bomber into enemy territory they would take a parachute, a pistol, a flare gun and some water purification tablets. A compass would be handy and a map too. They laughed and said that sort of planning was for military pilots and not business managers.

I ignored them.

Being prudent in the face of uncertainty I duly assembled my Personal Survival Kit.

Three days later, without warning, I was summoned before the personnel kraken to be dragged off the boat into the deep, cold waters of unemployment.

She patiently explained the leaky nature of the business, handed me a life jacket and suggested I went home and spent the weekend thinking of ways to stay on board the boat.

So having ruined my day, she wanted to ruin my weekend as well did she? I decided not to oblige her.

Instead, I reasoned with her that as the company was a multi-site, multi-million pound outfit they had probably already given some thought to my potential in other parts of the organization. I daringly suggested that if they really needed me we would be having a different conversation.

She smiled, guiltily, and waved a tentacle at me. Then we both agreed there were no other options, which at least saved me the hassle of spending the weekend convincing myself there was hope.

Whilst she was running through the rest of her bland script, I used the time to think.

What was my next step?

What did I need to do now?

The next step was to be spat out of her watery lair, back up to the sunlight of the office floor. My meerkat of a boss bought me a coffee, his nose twitching with anxiety, whilst he chatted about this and that. He was probably eyeing up the carpet for suitable spots to begin burrowing.

I ignored him and made a mental note of everything in my section that belonged to me.

When I had finished both my drink and my inventory, I left him twitching and walked over to my desk, where I pulled out my emergency plastic bag and calmly filled it with my gear. (It's surprising just how much you *cannot* fit into a brief case. A cheap supermarket bag takes up no space when stuffed in a desk drawer, or your brief case and is an essential bit of kit for use in emergency packing situations.)

A colleague looked over.

"Well done", he said. "We guessed you were being given a promotion."

"No", I replied. "I've been made redundant."

The shock on his face was palpable. If the supposed rising star could go, then anyone was fair game.

The need for a Personal Survival Kit suddenly became clear to him.

Annoyingly, that was the one day I had turned up for work early and was in and out so quickly my car engine was still warm. How unlucky can you get?

A second manager was despatched soon after, as I was enjoying the first rush of freedom down at the duck pond. His feathers were severely ruffled because it had happened without any warning.

What did he expect? A telegram with his breakfast cereal?

The first thing to do when considering some action is to do *nothing*. Start with some planning or you will rush headlong into the jaws of danger.

An old Zen proverb is your first port of call on the Cruise of Panic, calling in at the popular ports of Uncertainty, Bitterness and Resentment, the essence of which is:

"Don't do anything. Just sit tight and think."

Our natural response in stressful situations is either fight or flight. To do either effectively we have to plan a bit in advance. We know that our boss is an animal, lurking out there. We know the unexpected will happen, so there is no excuse for not organizing some sort of survival kit, however basic. Once you have prepared it, you will remember most of the contents when in a tight spot.

There is always more clutter to take home than you think and the best way to keep your inner health bubbling strongly is to make a clean sweep of your desk in one go.

I once saw a manager return to an office two weeks after his removal to collect his stapler. What a sad sap. Come back to pick up the office safe maybe, but not a stapler.

Instead the aim is to ride out of the office with your bags properly packed and your head held high.

Taking time to plan will help you to avoid increasing the chances of becoming an antelope on the Big Bad Day. When the big moment comes and you need something to hold on to, your Personal Survival Kit will help you stay a mature and rational person.

Use the planning process as a positive act from which to draw energy and to help reduce your stress levels. However dire your situation, some planning will reduce the uncertainties for you and your family. Less uncertainty equals less stress.

Having to face up to the reality of a tricky situation is always stressful and upsetting, however, if you take some time to focus on your strengths and your aspirations you will feel better in your self. Your confidence will increase because some of the uncertainty about the future will have been reduced.

If you generate some useful options that would involve moving you to a new role, or a new department in the same organization, you will have to pitch them to the company before you get shoved off the stern. Once the decision to lose you has been taken, people instantly get used to not having you around and you become the office ghost.

Remember: You are smart.

You have worth.

You have a brain and can use it. Thinking is work!

Planning will give you a sense of purpose because you are starting to assert your authority over the future.

Your bastard of a boss doesn't know you are planning, so you have an advantage over him.

Remember too, that the overall purpose is to ensure you pursue healthy behaviour, to keep evolving, to take maximum advantage of the situation, to ensure you have a fulfilling life and to increase your inner health.

You have already completed the first part of your Personal Survival Kit and have identified your Diamond Days and your key strengths and skills, so you have already begun the process. Hooray, a positive step already!

▌ **The next part is easy. You have already identified your most useful supporters.**
● **Are there any changes you would like to make? Could anybody help you to plan?**

Look again at your support group listed in your Personal Survival Kit and see if one of them is good at creating plans and options. If not, you may wish to add in someone who is good at this sort of thing.

Following on from that is the list of essential items that you will need to take with you, such as your water bottle and flare pistol.

You will have a surprising amount of gear scattered round your desk, your car, and the office environment.

Unless your stage name is The Amazing Antelope With The Marvellous Memory, you will not be able to think of it all in a hurry.

Do yourself a favour and in the peace and calm of an average day, write down all the bits and pieces you will take with you. Don't forget to include your coffee coaster or the loose change you keep in a tin at the bottom of a filing cabinet.

The little things can piss you off if you forget them, so don't feel silly about adding them to your list. If they are important to you then they are important. Full stop. Put them on the list.

Naturally, there's no need to include items that don't belong to you, theft is still theft, even in a panicky moment. And don't bring any matches or petrol cans. Torching the office could land you in deep trouble, particularly with the rest of the gang who will be jealous that you did it before them.

Aim to travel light.

Travel light and run fast. The vast majority of the files and notes that seem to have value are only of specific use to you in *that* role. Take them and they will only clutter up the attic. Leave them all behind and give yourself a better chance to break free of the past.

Always think about money due from holiday entitlements, back pay, maternity or paternity leave, overtime, bonuses, pension, or expenses. It is worth working out *precisely* what you think you are owed because companies can be notoriously slack in calculating it correctly. Don't rely on the personnel department to give you accurate information either. I mean if they could add up they'd be accountants, right?

> **!** **Have a think about it and then uncap your biro and complete Travelling**
> **●** **Light in your Personal Survival Kit (page 206). You may need to do some checking first, on the sly, or make sure your space on the holiday wall chart in the office is up to date. This could be the first place people look when calculating what you are owed. Be honest though, if you get caught fiddling things you could be dismissed.**

The other part of a good plan of action is the action bit itself.

What are you actually going to do?

Each type of animal can be countered in some form by appropriate behaviour on your part, but you will need to prepare in advance of an attack, when a wrong move could be disastrous.

If your strategy of camouflage, staying upwind, or staying out of the water has failed then you will need to give yourself the chance to reach the safety of your 4x4. Think about how you would handle a tricky situation. How will you feel in the heat of the moment? What would you like to say?

Rehearsal can be a superb method of reducing your stress levels.

If you were going to deliver a presentation to the board of directors you would rehearse it, so why not take ten minutes to run through your response for when you get ambushed, or summoned for a date with Madame Guillotine? Write down the actual words you will use and practice and polish them. For example, your response could be as simple as "I'll just get a coffee on the way, so see you in five minutes". This will buy you some time to fish out your Personal Survival Kit, or to head to the bathroom and compose yourself.

All four animals can be handled differently and preparation can help you to avoid sliding from a dignified adult into a helpless antelope. Sometimes it may be necessary for you to go to them, so don't wait to be ambushed. Get in there first.

Crocodiles are thoughtful creatures whose thinking processes happen out of sight. It is pointless trying to draw them into an instant decision as that will be viewed as an aggressive poke and they will bite back.

Give them some options to consider and make them feel they are an active part of the process. Do not force your views on them. Use assertive language and stand your ground.

A good tip with crocodiles, if you think they are going to attack, is to move to high ground. Hold your discussion in a neutral space, such as a general purpose meeting room because you need to see all of him to watch his body language.

You set the pace for the timing and location. Don't let him make any notes during the meeting, as you need him to listen to you. Use words such as *would*, or *feel* and ask questions in a calm, polite voice. These techniques help to keep you poised as an assertive adult and greatly reduce the chance that the crocodile will see you as an antelope. Emotional behaviour, swearing, or shouting all give your boss the green light to be mean to you. Try out:

"Would you consider these two options?"

"I feel that this is important to me."

"How do you see things going from here?"

"I feel that my strengths are x, y and z and would like you to consider a new role for me."

"I feel that having a daily review is not the only option and I would like to discuss ways of doing it differently."

"I feel confident that after completing this project I would be able to take on more taxing assignments..."

Asking questions is a good move. It will keep them talking and you may learn something. Crocs are stable and so will generally tell you things, if you ask in a non-aggressive manner. However, if they do snap at you, use the same breaking-off techniques that work with lions (below). Crucially, do not expect an answer to your questions at this meeting. End by agreeing the date of the next meeting, when you would like to receive his considered response.

Lions are stable like the crocodile and you should use a similar approach with your language. Words such as *think*, *should* and *ought* will all be seen as aggressive poking and will ensure you receive an aggressive response. Telling a lion that you think something is right simply invites them to argue back at you:

"Well, I think you're wrong. ROAR."

(The word *think* often implies rational logic and because in reality, logic is often muddled in with emotion, people can more easily challenge you on the detail of your thoughts. They can attempt to "out think" you. Hence the need to talk about your *feelings*, which you exclusively own.)

Lions are not to be argued with at all costs because they will whip out their cutlery and maul you for sport. A crocodile will slip back into the water and paddle off for a rethink, but a lion will damage you on the spot. Avoid arguments by sticking to your feelings, which are difficult to counter.

Be honest, but not inflammatory. Invite him to stick his emotions on hold for a moment. For example, you could open with:

"I would like to talk through my feelings about this subject. I would like to do so in a friendly and constructive way so that we can both move forwards."

The lion will be disarmed by your soothing overtones and will let you continue, interested in what you have to say. Then sketch out your feelings and suggest your solutions.

The lion will want to comment on your suggestions right away, so be prepared for this. Listen to what he has to say. He may be agreeing with you, but his confrontational style makes him want to win. He will need to show that it was his idea all along, so let him win. Letting him win means that you win. Winning is good. And if you must disagree then be positive about it:

"I hear what you have said and if we could include my earlier feelings we may be able to find a new solution, which is acceptable to both of us." (And if we do that I won't have to punch you on the snout.)

If a lion is starting to prepare an attack, he can be forced to break the move. An unexpected change of direction will throw him off his stride. Wait until he draws breath and then put your hand to your mouth, cough and say that you need to get a drink of water. Stand up and ask politely if he would like one as well? Once you have poured a drink, remain standing and take a sip. If he has remained seated, your height advantage will energise you. Think quickly: do you wish to continue, or do you wish to end the meeting to allow yourself time to regroup?

If you would like to stop, maintain the advantage you now have and suggest that as time is running on, you would like to pause at this point. You have some work to complete before the end of the day, or another meeting that you need to prepare for. Thank him for his support and suggest you reconvene later that day, or early tomorrow morning.

As you have broken his attack and he has lost the initiative he may well agree. If he doesn't, you can always insist:

"No, you bastard, I feel that I need some time to consider your comments."

If getting a drink is difficult, you can break the attack by excusing yourself to go to the bathroom, or by getting up and opening a window. Any small action that does not cause offence, but which forces him to drop his eye contact and prevents him from resuming the conversation is enough. Writing something down often works, not least because he thinks you are listening, when in reality you are planning your next move. Uncap your pen and say:

"Let me just write that down. I-am-a-useless-fuckwit. Hmm, interesting."

If you keep your head down and make copious notes, eventually he will stop talking and you can concentrate. It doesn't matter what you write because the essential healthy thing you can do is to have a rapid internal conversation and mentally run through your Personal Survival Kit.

If you are in doubt over how to begin your meeting it makes sense to outline a couple of your major issues and then ask for information from your boss. You may say something along the lines of:

"Now that I've explained my key feelings, please would you outline your future plans for the department? I may have misread the situation and am keen that we continue in the most productive fashion."

A lion will have a plan and may have already told you. A crocodile will have a plan, but will probably not have mentioned it. Seeking information is an assertive and healthy behaviour and will help you to formulate your strategy.

Elephants are emotional and you need to ensure that you do not startle them. Ask them for some time at their convenience and give them an outline agenda (as basic as possible). Do not rush at them with your issues, or your bucketful of solutions, as they will panic and trample you into the underlay.

Explain your feelings, offer them a couple of solutions and make it clear to them which one is your preferred option. Outline the advantages for both of you. Elephants will like this. Crocs and lions would hate this approach because it would sound patronising to them, as they like to work it out for themselves.

With an elephant you need to give them some time to digest your plan, but you may get an agreement in principle during the meeting. Being confrontational types they can make decisions very quickly, if you need one. Shut up for a minute and let them have a little think. Then ask them if they have any questions and repeat the advantages of your plan to them. For example:

"If I moved to the marketing department I would be able to support you when the need arose and this would save your department the cost of my salary." Or:

"If you let me have responsibility for the Mega project it would give Mrs Antelope more time to complete the annual stock audit."

You can ask an elephant for his strategy, but he probably won't have one. Instead ask him for his issues and concerns and he may reveal a few useful nuggets.

And if you should happen to cause him to panic and start to trample the room to bits, the best option is to feign a sudden emergency call on your mobile and leave in haste. Or you can drop your pen and hide under the desk, in an attempt to recover it.

Meerkats can be treated in a similar way to elephants, but they can be tricky little sods to pin down. They will not want to face up to you and may even make it worse by chatting through their fears about your request with a colleague, which could cause a lion to amble into your life.

Corner them by matching your timetable with theirs and suggest a meeting at the start, or end of the day, whichever suits them best. The office will be quieter and they will be less skittish. Try to arrange the meeting away from their desk so they cannot hide behind bits of paper, or make phone calls. Remind them that you wish to have a friendly chat and that you need their assistance.

Meerkats will worry about what you have to say, in case it will cause them trouble. For example, they may try to talk you out of resigning because that would mean having actively to do something about managing the department. They will not like that. They may even fob you off with things like:

"Oh that can wait a little while. It's not important right now."

It jolly well is. Or:

"Tell you what, let's carry on as we are for six months and then we can talk again."

Nothing will change and you will have wasted half a year.

Meerkats need deadlines to work to. Ask them if they would like one week, or two weeks to decide. Being non-confrontational they will need to have a little internal chat with themselves and the choice will help them to feel secure and will remove the surprise element, which they hate.

As with an elephant, a meerkat will need your guidance and you will have to remind them how they can benefit from your plan. They will not be interested in the advantages to you. They have too many worries of their own to attend to before considering your issues.

If a meerkat starts digging a hole, keep him focused on your issues and the need for them to be resolved. You may have to hang onto his tail to stop the little bugger from slipping away to safety.

> **❗ In your Personal Survival Kit, complete Dealing with my Boss (page 207).**
> **● Include the new behaviour which you are going to practice with your animal-boss. You may wish to flick back to the field research to see if there are any other options worth adding in. Apply some common sense and feel free to mix and match options to suit particular situations. There is a summary of "how to" pointers at the end of this chapter, so you may like to read on, have a think and then come back to this later.**

The stress of a crunchy situation can be overwhelming.

Even though you know full well that you are not the first or the last person to go through tough times, stress can shred your poise and quickly reduces confident, assertive professionals to quivering wrecks.

Having a handful of competencies is unlikely to help when your stomach has turned into a washing machine, you need to run to the loo, or your sweaty hands have started to smudge your notes. However, there are some quick and useful routines that you can learn to help get a grip on yourself when you feel your feet sliding towards the gaping jaws of a raging beast.

Getting a grip (sometimes known as *grounding*) enables you to regain some control over your inner self and helps you to retain a healthy perspective on the situation before you. It involves distracting your urge to fight or flight in order to break the cycle of negative action and reaction, which can suck you in, mash you about and spit you out in an instant.

Have a look through the following list of suggestions. Practise the first one and then choose a couple of spares which most appeal to you:

1. **Take three deep breaths.** Breathe in through your nose, feel your lungs expand, hold for a count of ten and then breathe out slowly through your mouth. In through your nose–hold–out through your mouth. Notice how you feel calmer already. This exercise works because you interrupt the release of adrenaline and force your brain to slow down your pulse. (Only

do what you feel comfortable with and never fly in the face of medical advice with this one. For example, if you suffer from shortness of breath, then you may wish to consult a doctor first. Remember that you shall remain responsible for your actions, so use a bit of common sense.)

2. **Notice the environment you are in.** Is it hot or cold? What can you smell? What shapes and colours are pleasing to you?

3. **Look down at your notes and count the number of words in each sentence.** Look at the loops in your handwriting. Notice how consistent they are.

4. **Hold your hands below the table, out of sight.** Grip the wrist of your writing hand, then relax and stroke the skin on the outside edge of that hand. How does it feel?

5. **Imagine you are in a fancy restaurant, with food in front of you.** What would you have as a starter? What would it smell like? Taste your first mouthful.

6. **Imagine you are sitting on a warm sunny beach.** Concentrate on listening to the sound of the surf. Feel the sand between your toes. What colour is your towel?

7. **Remember where you were before you worked for this company.** Recall the face of a previous colleague who made you laugh. Remind yourself that there is a future beyond your current situation.

8. **Take notes.** Use the opportunity of writing to break eye contact and to create some thinking space.

9. **Arrange your posture.** Make a conscious effort to sit in a more balanced way. If you are leaning forwards, putting your head on one side or pursing your lips, you are probably starting to look aggressive. Instead, sit back in your chair, straighten your back and put your hands in your lap. Keep your head straight and relax your jaw so that you're not clenching your teeth.

10. **Think about what you will say to your partner on your return from work.** Will you be telling them about how you kept cool and didn't lose your temper? Run through the conversation in your head. Feel the pride of maintaining your professional dignity.

Grounding techniques can really help you to maintain a healthy inner balance, which in turn can increase the chances of retaining a mature perspective and avoiding becoming an antelope shaped victim. Most of us have, at some point, "lost it" in the heat of the moment and lived to regret our outburst. There is no lasting satisfaction from a moment of carelessness, or childish behaviour. You will lose dignity and then be attacked from all sides:

"You'll never guess what Darwin did? Completely lost it! Bounced off the walls and then blew out like a tornado. His giant tortoise is in a right state!"

Your ex-colleagues will all cluck in agreement at the stupidity of your actions and because only stupid people do stupid things, you will have given your boss the green light to carrying on with his plan. You have just legitimized his strategy and proved that he was right all along:

"We always knew he was too emotional to be a truly good accountant."

! **To help you in a tough spot, please**
choose and practice your preferred
● grounding techniques. Then turn to
your Personal Survival Kit and complete
Grounding Techniques (page 208).

Many people fail to do any planning and they leap into the unknown without even a handkerchief in their pockets. They increase the risk of disaster by several hundred percent, so if you've skimmed through this chapter you may wish to go round again. On the other hand, if you have been paying attention, then you've thought about the behaviour your boss may exhibit and have some coping strategies in your Personal Survival Kit.

If you are pitching to your bastard of a boss think about his wild animal status and *how* you can help to get yourself into a good position.

Crocodiles are best approached on neutral ground, so arrange for a meeting away from his office. Give him time to think about your comments by arranging a follow-up meeting. Explain how your ideas fit in with his plan and leave some room for him to contribute to the discussion.

Lions like to eat meat, so start your meeting by reminding him of all your successes and how you have added value and generally done a good job. He will need to be reminded and a positive start will help to avoid an early mauling. Lions are always on the look out for confrontation so use language which invites him to think, such as "I would like you to consider this", or "what ideas do you have?"

Some of these approaches can be mixed and matched between lions and crocodiles, so apply common sense here and avoid inflaming their passion. You will need both legs to drive home with.

Elephants need to be treated gently. When arranging your meeting emphasize that you would like a friendly and positive discussion. Choose a time when the elephant is at his most docile, perhaps at the end of the day when the telephones have stopped ringing. Soothe him with hot coffee and offer him an agenda to look at in advance. Stay calm and keep smiling to avoid him getting emotional.

Meerkats, unlike elephants, need to be treated more firmly. Grab his tail and nail it to the desk. Practically speaking this means asking clear questions and keeping your sentences short and precise. Be prepared for him to answer a different question to the one you have asked. Listen patiently, ignore his reply and then repeat your question. This approach will keep him focused on you and your needs. End the meeting with a commitment for action and make sure he agrees to a mutually satisfactory timescale.

Clearly meerkats and elephants both need to feel secure. You may find it helpful to thank them for their support at the start of the meeting as this courtesy will help them to feel more comfortable with their surroundings. Thanking them may sound appalling, if they are appalling, but we are aiming for survival here and effort is needed.

We also now know the items that we cherish and need to take, if we find ourselves moving on and we have some techniques up our sleeve to keep us safe when our boss makes his move.

We can now move on and bump into options.

People like options. Having options gives you choices and people like choices.

Imagine when your dream date buys you a box of chocolates for Valentine's Day. You open them, full of anticipation, but stare in horror at the lines of identical brown lumps. No choice?

No fun.

A box of chocolates should contain lots of lovely, different centres, all decorated in artful patterns. Hazelnut whirls, lemon ices, strawberry centres, choca-mocha blocks and coconut crunch crumbles should all be present and correct. If your true love gave you a box of "Same Centres" you would think that it was time to put an advert in the lonely-hearts column of your local paper:

"Fun professional type, with own hair and GSOH, seeks same for friendship and broad-minded chocolate pleasure. Hard centres a speciality. Send photo of box."

We all have choices and we always have more than may be apparent at first glance.

So now that we have taken some time to stop and think about our boss and the ways he may behave and have planned the items to take and have chosen our preferred grounding techniques, we can think about the positive steps we are going to take for ourselves.

10

Options, Options Everywhere...
Set sail for the future

We may not realize how many things we can do and how many paths there are to choose from. If we're under stress our thinking gets narrowed and we may lock ourselves into a course of action without considering other possibilities. It's only when we're looking back over our shoulder some months later that we sigh and say:

"If only I had thought to do that, instead! What an idiot I've been!"

As you read through the suggested options below, try to avoid dismissing any of them out of hand, because if you hear yourself saying "I would never do that", you may be motivated more by fear than by practical considerations. It's okay to be a bit worried and that's a good sign that you are a regular human being. Discuss things with your friends, or your partner and they will be able to give you an objective perspective.

And now, drum roll please, here come some options for you to ponder.

1. **Our first choice for our new future can be to stop doing something.** To get ourselves into a groovy new position the first step is probably to stop doing those bits and pieces that are sapping our energy. Do you work late and spend an hour on a routine task that would take you five minutes in the morning when you are fresh? Do you grumble at the kids, or moan all the time to your partner? Do you duck the issue and convince yourself that today is not the right time, but tomorrow will be a fresh start? The first thing to stop is probably the little reward you have each day to make up for your difficult work environment. An extra biscuit at tea break? A double gin at lunchtime? They are not doing you any good. Stop rewarding yourself for inaction, or at least have a splash of tonic with the gin. Instead, wake up to the fact that something is going to have to change. Stop hiding under the corporate duvet and acknowledge that you're in Shit Street. Then reward yourself for waking up.

2. **The next option is to go and meet your bastard of a boss.** Once you have woken up it can be immensely rewarding to tackle the problem head on. If you and he both know there is a dead fish under your desk, you may as well take it into his office and discuss what to do about it. Think about the options described in the previous chapter about how to set up and conduct a meeting, then plan for success, practise and go for

it. Remember to list all the things which you have done well, as it helps to increase the strength of your position by reminding him of all your successes. Your boss will probably have overlooked all of them, so a timely reminder is essential. Most wild animals can be surprisingly meek when faced with someone who takes the fight to them and although you may accelerate the process of change, at least you will have also reduced the number of days you will have to fret about it. That's a pretty good payoff for you and your family, who will probably be as keen (and as nervous) as you to sort things out.

3. **A more radical option you have is to leave.** You can always vote with your feet, if you want to. The door to the outside world is always there to be used and given the way society is becoming increasingly job-mobile the chances are that you'll find another gig to keep you in gin and biscuits. You always have that option, and if you want to leave then a bit of forward planning can make it sweeter. Keep your powder dry, sort out your domestic affairs, type up a fresh curriculum vitae (CV) or résumé, start looking for another source of income and then when you are ready, resign. You won't be the first and you won't be the last.

4. **If you want a change of direction you can leave and set up your own business, or go and do further education.** Simply swapping one job for another

may not be enough to get you back on the right path. Many people enjoy working for themselves, perhaps using their trade skills, or as a consultant, or facilitator. To help reach a higher rung on the corporate ladder it can be fun to go and do some further training. Taking time out to top up your learning may be the tonic you need to give your career a boost. People who continue to learn and develop themselves can be the ones who really have a happy and productive working life.

5. **Alternatively you can stay, but stay differently.** This can mean physically relocating to a new department, or staying at your old desk and changing roles, or simply asking for that juicy project that always eludes you. It's surprising what you can get by asking and, as the saying goes: "If you don't ask then the answer is always *no!*" Many bosses would rather you transferred than left, because each staff member lost does eventually count against them. To lose one member of staff is unfortunate. To lose two is careless. To lose three starts to mire them in political poo. Everything has its consequences.

6. **You can ask for assistance.** Asking for help is okay and there is no disgrace in owning up to a blank spot in your education or competencies. State your issues and outline where you feel you could improve, if you had some training or support. This could be as simple as having regular monthly management reviews to

help keep you focused. Sadly, many people don't talk with their boss often enough. Their boss sets annual objectives and leaves them to it without checking their understanding, or their motivation to achieve them. He may be a bastard, but your boss can't read your mind, so if you need to discuss things with him, you'll need to actually tell him this. Confront the animal you know your boss to be and arrange a meeting.

7. **You can ask for some external support.** If your boss is difficult to talk to you can always ask him to pay for third party support from a mentor or a coach. Our stress levels could be greatly reduced if we all had space and time to talk confidentially to someone every month. To ask silly questions of, to rehearse our suggested plans with and to help us develop our positive behaviour patterns. If you were a top athlete would you have a personal coach to guide you, or would you train yourself?

8. **One option is to ask for voluntary redundancy.** It may be obvious that you are going to be made redundant, so you have an opportunity to try and leave on your terms. Be careful with this option though. You do not want to accidentally resign, as a miserable dung beetle of a boss will snap up your offer and toss you aside like a used tissue. So make it clear that you would be open to offers, but are not tendering your resignation. Many bosses hate the bad press they attract

from a redundancy situation, so this can give them an opportunity to make you redundant and announce it in such a way that looks like you resigned. This will avoid the fake sympathy your colleagues would have given you. Instead they are full of respect that you have made the big decision and unknown to them you have a fat cheque to help you celebrate with your ego.

9. **If you have a serious issue with your boss, then have a go at complaining.** Don't go to your boss, but seek out someone higher up the chain and state your case. Make sure you have reasonable grounds because undermining your boss is a great way to get yourself rushed straight to the top of the "Gits to be sacked" list. To ensure your case is heard it's vital to collect some objective evidence of his status as a true bastard. Jot down notes when bad things happen and best of all collect direct quotes. These can be very effective as evidence of his poor behaviour and if genuinely recorded with details of the time, date and situation can be difficult to brush aside. And it's fun to quote someone's ill-judged remarks back to them in front of their senior manager. Once your grievance is underway, many companies will tread carefully to avoid being held up for constructive dismissal. If you really feel there is a proper complaint to be heard then you may wish to consider this. It is your right after all. Remember too, that if you suddenly find yourself being made redundant, you often have an automatic

right of appeal, which can time-expire. Some companies can be slack in telling you your rights. Make sure you know the procedure for raising your grievance and always stick rigidly to the company's procedures to avoid a technical knock out.

10. **A cautious approach can be a great first step when sizing up your options.** Do nothing obvious. Sit back, plan your future, think about your wider career aspirations. Bring your CV up to date*, complete your Personal Survival Kit, but don't confront your boss. Just sit back and wait and see what develops. Be the researcher in the Serengeti. Make notes and observe what is going on around you. Draw your own conclusions and think hard about your Diamond Days. If you're lucky you may be made redundant and have the chance of a fulfilling life elsewhere. Doing nothing can be a productive strategy to help you make sense of a rotten situation. It's also a positive choice, as you are choosing to take this course of inaction.

11. **If you're not sure what to do first and want to release some bottled up emotions keep a diary of events, or write a report for yourself.** Write down everything that has happened to you and capture all of your feelings. If you're angry this is a great safety valve

---

* For more detail about CV writing, including worked examples and how to add value, please refer to the book *Job Hunting 3.0*

to blow off some steam. Don't self-edit when you're writing, just bash it all down and keep on writing (or typing) until you've pulled the sting and have let the poison work itself out of your system. This will give you something to do, which is a low risk activity and can generate high rewards, in terms of emotional satisfaction. You also then have the benefit of reading your notes, which will support your thinking and your decision making will be sharper for having removed some of the clouds in your head.

The options suggested above are there to get your thinking started. Feel free to invent new ones, or to mix and match ideas to concoct your preferred plan of action. Invite your support group to listen to your intentions and ask them to test your thinking, in order to uncover any assumptions you have made.

Before you choose which option grabs your attention (you can trust your intuition), here they are again, stripped down to the headlines:

1. Our first choice for our new future can be to stop doing something.
2. The next option is to go and meet your bastard of a boss.
3. A more radical option you have is to leave.
4. If you want a change of direction you can leave and set up your own business, or go and do further education.
5. Alternatively you can stay, but stay differently.
6. You can ask for assistance.

7. You can ask for some external support.
8. One option is to ask for voluntary redundancy.
9. If you have a serious issue with your boss, then have a go at complaining.
10. A cautious approach can be a great first step when sizing up your options.
11. If you're not sure what to do first and want to release some bottled up emotions keep a diary of events, or write a report for yourself.

> **! ● Think about the options which most appeal to you and then turn to your Personal Survival Kit and complete Tomorrow is a Fresh Start (page 209). Write down your choices and at least one thing which you will do to help one of them become a reality. It's positive action that counts. Put down what your heart desires and trust your judgement.**

Regardless of whichever option you choose as a starting point, one of the key tools you will need for the future is a silky smooth personal career summary. Preferably about you and your many achievements and not about your holiday spent clubbing in Ibiza, or the time you and a bunch of champagne quaffing account executives got drunk and pinched a policeman's helmet.

Writing a career résumé or a curriculum vitae can be boring, but it does focus the mind and these things can be surprisingly difficult to put together after you have left. Once outside the corporation gates your memory will fade fast, so put in the effort whilst you can easily check facts and ponder your successes.

CV formats can change with fad, fashion and location, so make sure yours is up to date, is accurate and has no spelling mistakes. Remove all cheesy clip art, lavish fonts and gimmicks. Never ever print it out on lavender scented paper. If it takes up more than two pages you need to prune it back so it fits.

Your key *successes* or *achievements* must leap off the page and not sit in the corner sucking their thumbs. When did you stamp your mark on the business? What drew the highest praise or made a tangible difference to business performance? Always include some numbers, as they are easy to remember and they show the scale of your achievement.

Think of yourself as a product. You are marketing and selling yourself to people who have never heard of you and who care more about their lunch than about you. Your CV has to do the same job as a product brochure. Who would buy you? What sort of things will make them want to part with their hard-earned cash? What will make you stand out from a pile of 500 CVs?

You need to be clear, interesting, relevant and informative. A good test to ensure you are not filling your CV with spurious or vague achievements is to ask *so what* of each of them. For example, if you wrote "I managed a team", then ask, *so what?* If your answer is; "we increased output by 50 per cent", then that's the bit that needs to be in your CV.

Also include some information about *how* you did it, to show which tools or techniques you used and to make it clear that you have depth. Some examples of achievements could include:

- Developed the service team, which improved our customer retention by 20% through the use of disgracefully intrusive psychometric testing.
- Won three new contracts, worth a total of £10m per annum, by being the smoothest snake in the reptile house.
- Installed a slick packing process which improved profits by 5% over two years. This was based on Professor Pant's model of Integrated Irrelevance.
- Trained up five new starters in how to use the coffee machine. Mine's an espresso.
- Made it to first base with the flirt in marketing Yummy.

Don't let your ego put in any flaky achievements of dubious worth, as you need to focus on quality and not quantity. Try and limit yourself to between six and ten achievements for your current position and have only two to four for each previous role. This approach can shine more light on your most recent (or most relevant) experience. Exercise a bit of judgement when deciding what to put in, or leave out. Leaving things out does not waste them. Keep them in reserve to blast away your interviewer, who will impressed that your CV was a just a *sample* of your achievements.

People will often decide on your suitability within 30 seconds of taking your CV out of the envelope, so don't fool yourself that they will be sitting there with a coffee and a cream cake, chortling over your amusing anecdotes. How much of your CV can you read in 30 seconds? Time yourself. It's not long to make an impression.

Also, many CVs are now scanned for key words. If an employer is looking for a "Blond-haired, brown-eyed, muscle-bound Viking, with his own battleaxe", then it can help to include some of these words in the first couple of lines. If you include all possible key words you could look like a weird genetic management experiment, so be thoughtful about it and go for the ones that are most in line with your experience and aspirations.

Remember your ego? He'll want you to include all sorts of adjectives which paint you in a great light, but be warned. Someone who describes themself as:

"A natural born leader with kicking communication skills, able to think inside and outside the box, with a detailed big-picture approach, amazing stamina and a reputation for delivering hot wet kisses to order..."

... might just be over doing things a *tiny weeny* bit. Choose three key adjectives and remember the old maxim:

"If it sounds too good to be true, it probably is."

Once you have two pages of cracking CV it's worth reducing them to a single summary sheet, to chuck out the chaff.

Drop off all the really old jobs, or the lame training courses that don't add anything. If you had eight key achievements whittle them down to five. Fewer, but higher grade, achievements present a much stronger case. Be ruthless and focus on the things that will help you to make the move that will bring you fulfilment. Once you have a single sheet résumé, take a fresh look at your two-page CV. There may be some more pruning and tweaking needed to sharpen it up even more.

If your CV was food, would it be an unappetizing bowl of ducks' feet soup? Or a plate of sexy grilled sea bass? Give it to a friend to read and ask them for their comments. If they take too long in answering it means that they're trying to think of something to say which won't hurt your feelings too much. This means it's duck feet soup for you. Do some more filleting and try again.

Once you have a CV, you may still wish to do nothing. That's cool because doing nothing can sometimes be the smart move. You may know your boss, but you may not be tapped into the politics above him. If a corporate lion mauls him, you may be up for promotion. Stick around, but don't stick to the floor. Discreetly gather information and review your plans with every new twist and turn.

Stay on the ball and take a swig of water from your water bottle to help keep yourself grounded.

If you do decide to set off on a journey you need to have your objective in clear sight. You need to know what the likely outcome will be. A handy phrase to have in your pocket at this point is:

"If you don't know where you're going then all roads lead there."

Darwin did not join the HMS Beagle because he was fed up with having to wait 160 years for satellite television. He wanted to learn, because learning would help his career. His outcome was *knowledge*, and for that he was prepared to put up with ship's biscuits, weevils and lonely sailors.

The outcome is the big bit. The thing that most people avoid most of the time, because it means facing up to reality and accepting that you need to make changes and have to EVOLVE.

You have a choice. You always have a choice. Would you like to stop now, or would you like to carry on and take a small risk?

The risk is that you will have to be honest with yourself and you will have to face up to that honesty. What will be on your tombstone?

"Mrs Antelope died here. Unfulfilled and longing for a better life." Prepare yourself.

Make a milky drink, or crack open a beer. Open a box of delicious chocolates, or munch on your favourite biscuits. You need an energy boost to sustain you because facing up to your deep-down-needs can be tiring. Then put on some favourite music, to blot out the sound of everyday life and to inspire your thinking.

When you are ready, read through the following list of questions, answering each one in turn. The questions are designed to help you focus your thinking. There is no monopoly on groovy questions, so feel free to add in your own special ones, if they would help you to make progress.

You may find it useful to write things down. Capture your initial thoughts, because they are likely to be the most truthful ones and write them down exactly as they come to you, word for word. Don't be tempted to edit them before they've even reached the page, as that would be cheating.

What outcomes do you need, to ensure you have a fulfilling life and to keep your inner health glowing? Chew over the following questions, at a steady loping pace and don't panic if you can't answer all of them in one go. One good question with one honest answer is a great start to future fulfilment.

Desired Outcome Questions

1. How happy do I feel today? On a scale from 1 to 10 (where 1 is Shitty and 10 is on Top of the World) where do I sit? What single thing would move me up the scale by one point?
2. When were my last two Diamond Days?
3. Which tasks give me the greatest pleasure?
4. Would I like to try something different? A bit different, or radically different?
5. Where would I really like to live?
6. What do I need to do in the immediate future? Talk to my partner? See the bank manager? Finish the chocolates?
7. How much money do I need to earn? Is this true, or is my ego talking? What is the minimum I need each month to survive?

8. What financial support do I need to have in place? Who could help with this?

9. Where could I be in six months if I really went for it? Do I have a burning ambition that is eating me up and needs to be satisfied?

10. What is holding me back? Is it my ego, surfing again? What am I afraid of? The possibility of failure? Or of being ridiculed by my peers for having a dream and wanting to follow it?

11. What am I prepared to sacrifice to get what I really want?

12. What really matters to my family and me? Good health? A bigger car? More fulfilling leisure time?

13. What does my ideal family life look like? (Have fun writing down a timetable for a really satisfying week).

14. Whom do I use as a role model for my future work? What have they done which is inspirational?

15. What is my vision of the future which I can picture in my mind's eye? What is the ultimate outcome after the next five years that I would take in an instant today, if my fairy godmother flew in and turned a bowl of spicy noodles into my dream job?

All of these questions involve risk.

The risk that your dream is somehow foolish and that people will laugh at you, that success may take longer than you anticipated, or that the road ahead is full of potholes. These risks are the same for everyone. With proper planning and some careful thought, risks can be mitigated and turned from scary giants into tame little mice.

A group of friends met for their annual summer barbecue and chatted about their jobs and what they would really like to do. It transpired that each person was secretly beavering away on their own little project. They shared their dreams and their plans and nobody laughed, so they shared information on a regular basis and supported each other whenever possible.

This reduced the risks for each of them, because they respected each other's dreams. They all had dreams. People who worked to make theirs a reality were at the top of the social heap and tapped into a ready supply of support, which until they shared their dream, they did not realize was there for the taking.

It is important to think carefully about what you are prepared to sacrifice to reach your dream. And pay some attention to what your nearest and dearest are prepared to throw into the pot as well.

Sacrifices can be large or small, tangible or intangible. Cars are large and mobile phones are small. Pension contributions and holiday entitlement are tangible, as are reduced meals, or cheap flights.

Intangible things may be the routine that goes on at home, or the pleasure derived from chatting to a long established business contact. Social status is intangible because you can't touch it, but you can touch the drinks which you scoffed at posh parties and the times when you pigged out at the corporate trough.

Simply being "The Manager" is an intangible benefit which can be hard to leave behind, although we are never as important as we think we are. Good business was carried on before we arrived and will continue unabated in our absence.

You may need to sacrifice some of your ego, admit that you don't know everything there is to know about the universe and take up some extra training. You may even wish to sacrifice your whole career and start over. Experience itself is never sacrificed, only technical knowledge, which is often only relevant to a specific point in space and time. Look around your office at the files you never touch and the items you have kept "just in case" and never seem to need.

Stepping away from old knowledge and embracing the new can be tremendously liberating and energy giving, if it is taking you towards your goal.

One of the more positive spin-offs of the increasingly short time people spend in a particular job is a ready acceptance that you can change careers several times. People are often not hugely interested in what you did ten years ago, as long as it wasn't to start a ten-stretch for armed robbery.

If you feel stuck in a rut and wish to go and do something wildly different you can cash in on society's more relaxed approach to a modern career path. Employers are more likely to focus on your recent achievements, than to worry you haven't been steeped in their industry since you were knee high to a grasshopper.

Good people are hard to find and good learners who genuinely evolve and adapt are a rare and valuable commodity. Smart people, who are the ones who employ smart people, appreciate this and can see the added value in hiring someone who is mad keen to keep learning. This is because these people are better placed to help the organization move forwards.

Caution is needed here. Reflection without any action usually results in navel gazing and stagnation, so don't let Father Time sneak up and smack you round the back of the head, because he's a hard hitter.

The timescale of your current situation must be kept in sight.

How much time do you have before you will be forced to make a decision or take the first step? Do you have days, or weeks to plan? Sometimes you will have hours, or only a token ten minutes to clear your desk and hit the streets.

> Have a look through your list of answers to the previous questions. What leaps out at you? What makes your heart sing and your mouth stretch into an impish smile? Then turn to your Personal Survival Kit and fill out My Desired Outcomes (page 210). Don't worry if you are unable to complete all the boxes. Just fill in the bits which have value to you now. You can always come back and add in more detail when you're ready.

Then fill out My Dream Outcome (page 211) to focus your thinking towards one clear aspiration. What would you really, really like to have a go at? What is the role, or specialization, that you secretly wish you were doing right now? It's okay to have ambitions and it can inspire you to make progress by acknowledging them.

Having completed that, you should now have a much better understanding of your desires, ambitions and outcomes needed to turn your personal crankshaft, so that the spluttering engine of your career bursts into life.

Don't shed any tears if you only have part of the picture. That's still an impressive start over the rest of the herd.

You also have a rough guide to understanding your boss. This will help you tailor your behaviour to communicate positively and avoid becoming crocodile fodder, a lion's dinner, or something an elephant just trod on. Or it will help out, should you find yourself stranded helplessly next to the burrow of a meerkat, with a broken leg and a posse of vultures nibbling your butt.

Options, options everywhere... all around us, waiting for us to pick them up and start working towards our new life.

Choosing an option and putting it into action will take you towards your desired future and away from your animal of a boss. Don't flinch from reality and instead use your support group to ensure they keep you facing square onto the situation.

Keep in sight how much *time* you have to set your affairs in order and think about what is driving the situation forwards?

Plan ahead to ensure you remain in control of your feelings and actions. Smart people will work hard to remain in control during the difficult moments and then will find safe ways of releasing their emotion afterwards.

What outcomes do you seek in the long term? What will you stop doing tomorrow in order to take one positive step towards a better future?

Retain your dignity at all times. This is healthy behaviour that will help you to keep your spirits up and remain positive. Rehearse a couple of grounding techniques, to avoid a fist fight when a bastard boss throws a bucket of cold water over you, or starts a meeting by slapping a pair of thumb screws on the table.

Enjoy the thrill of the ride and when you get fed up, do something about it.

There are always more rides to go on.

And now that you are bit more prepared, the risky rides may not look quite as daunting as they did at first sight.

You have learned something about yourself and your environment.

You are smart and we're almost finished.

There is however, one little tip left to top up your learning with.

11

You're a Sun Beam Dude
Thank you and goodnight

The rain is rapidly turning from a downpour into a dribble.

The world is drying out fast.

You feel a bit stuffy now and are keen to pull on some shoes, run outside to breathe the cool, fresh air and enjoy the intoxicating rush of that delicious after-the-storm tang.

By using your insights you will be able to maintain a healthy attitude and practice more positive behaviour. You will be able to decide for yourself what is hurting you and what you will actually *do* about it.

You have greatly reduced your chances of becoming a tasty antelope and although you may still have a bastard for a boss, you are already several steps forward from when you started reading this book.

You are now ready to escape, if you want to! Ready to go under the wire and make a break for the trees before the searchlights snap onto you.

Go for it!

Run for your life!

However, at this point you may be hesitant, steeling yourself for the moment when you jump into the future. This, by its nature, can be the most terrifying part of the whole adventure. Like the seconds when a parachutist is poised in the doorway of a small, wobbly plane with 10,000 feet between him and a safe landing. Do you jump, or do you stay on board?

One little tip that separates the **movers** from the **stayers** is the way they *visualize* the future. If you can see a huge pile of work and you feel bogged down by the enormity of the task you are probably going to stay as *stuck* as a truck with a flat tyre.

Instead, visualize the world *after* the work has been done and capture the positive feelings of warmth, joy and success that come flooding in. Close your eyes then picture the scene and *feel* your heart soar into the clouds.

This is easily practised.

Think about a piece of work, or a task you are struggling to start. Then stand up and close your eyes. Now concentrate on generating a picture of the finished work, perhaps it is a completed report, or a cupboard you have tidied up. Look hard at the finished item and feel yourself smile with the pleasure of a job well done. Notice how you feel full of positive energy and are keen to celebrate your success. When you have captured these feelings, open your eyes, take a step forward and start work on the task you have been delaying.

You are now a **mover** and will be able to take a small step to help yourself.

So stand up again and this time, think about just your first *small* step towards future fulfilment. What is the first thing that you are going to do?

Some sample options include:

1. Having a serious talk with your partner.
2. Ringing your boss to arrange *that* meeting.
3. Completing a task that has been annoying your boss.
4. Going to see the bank manager.
5. Meeting with someone who is where you *want* to be and asking them for advice.
6. Drawing a picture of your new world.
7. Getting a brochure for the training you would like to do.
8. Writing down your list of comments to be discussed with your boss.
9. Going out for dinner to celebrate your strengths and your successes.
10. Noting down the *actual* words you will use to start the meeting with your boss.
11. Registering your CV with a recruitment agency.
12. Telling your best friend that you would like to discuss your ideas with them.
13. Taking a long walk to give you some thinking space.
14. Researching your new career aspirations.
15. Talking to a professional third party supporter, such as a coach or mentor.

When you have decided on this first small, safe step, capture the feelings of joy and pleasure this action will bring you. Then open your eyes, take a step forwards and...

! ... Turn to your Personal Survival Kit and complete My First Step (page 212). What are you going to do? Which action will set the wheels in motion for you? Then choose a reward.

After that, complete My CV (page 213). Exercise some honest judgement here. There's no need to pitch for perfection. Good enough is all we need. Once you have circled the points put a strong plastic bag in your briefcase, or desk drawer for emergency packing. Plastic bags can be surprisingly difficult to find in a crisis at work and if you do need to use it, you can feel suitably smug that you were prepared.

Then, when you are satisfied proceed straight to Honesty Check (page 214).

When that has been completed leap over the finish line, punch the air with glee and complete Celebration (page 215).

Well done!

You now have a useful tool that will help you to navigate through troubled waters. Your Personal Survival Kit is complete and you have faced up to reality. It's worth reflecting on the fact that the emotional satisfaction people enjoy from learning and evolving helps to sustain them through periods of fear, uncertainty and momentary panic.

Take a moment to run through some grounding techniques again, to practise them. Take a deep breath, or feel the warm, soft sand between your toes, or smell the delicious food your imagination has served up.

Learn and laugh. Feel the benefits of making progress and enjoy your past errors and pitfalls. You'll learn to love laughing.

Remember why you are doing it all.

Remember why you came home and screamed out:

"I hate my job!", or

"I'm so stressed!", or

"My boss is a COMPLETE BASTARD!"

And why you wanted to weep with frustration, and hurt and fear.

You are your own person. You are smart and your skills and talents are still with you and will survive these trying times.

Be aware of your environment and of your ambitions. Behave with dignity and maturity, use appropriate language and take control of a tricky situation.

Don't become an antelope.

When your boss turns into a cunning crocodile, a leaping lion, an emotional elephant or a missing meerkat, appraise his likely actions and react accordingly. Develop your repertoire of positive behaviour and respond intelligently to his moves, so that your inner health remains intact and survives any knocks.

Use assertive language that includes non aggressive comments such as; "I feel that…" and "Would you consider …"

Always ask questions, seek clarity and don't be afraid to ask your boss for his vision of the future. The outcome may still be the same from his perspective, but you will retain your dignity and your health. You will start the next slice of your life journey from a stronger position than if you had allowed yourself to be slung into a mud-filled ditch.

The world turns and you have a choice. You can choose productive behaviour and can play to your strengths.

You do not have to like the fact that the world has turned.

But you need to turn with it, because turning with the world makes you a LEARNER and learners EVOLVE and stride up mountains.

Learners also avoid being roughed up by the wild animals and sometimes get to go home with that attractive flirt in the marketing department.

Hooray for learners!

They enjoy rich, fulfilling experiences that satisfy their soul and keep their inner health strong. Don't muck about ducking and diving and avoiding the crunchy issues. You are only robbing yourself of the opportunity to do something about it, which is a shame.

You have *one* life and you are in charge of it, so give yourself some leadership, because it's all about you and your behaviour.

We all choose our behaviour and we need to make positive choices.

The rain has stopped, the sun is waving at you and it's going to be a beautiful day.

The world looks glorious and the dusty, dangerous Serengeti is far away. You now know where you are and what you intend to do about it. You're a happy Sunbeam Dude, with a smile on your face and hope in your heart.

Enjoy your day.

Laugh and learn.

Have fun.

Evolve and be fulfilled.

12

Your Personal Survival Kit
Cut out and keep safe

The end of the book has arrived. The only thing left do is read through your Personal Survival Kit and make any changes or additions.

Then cut it out and keep it somewhere safe and accessible. Type it into your PDA if you want to be flash, but always keep a hard copy in case of unexpected battery failure, or sudden contact with a concrete floor.

Keep it locked away from the prying eyes of your boss and your colleagues.

Trust nobody in the office, because you really don't know who is licking the earlobe of your boss behind closed doors. And given that he's a stinking animal, whose idea of a bath is to roll in the dust, they're welcome to lick away.

They may even chance an intimate nibble from time to time and if they know about your Personal Survival Kit, then it's sure to creep into the conversation.

As it's *your* kit, keep it to yourself at work.

Invite your partner and your trusted supporters to have a look, even to celebrate your strengths and your new found sense of purpose.

Crack open a bottle of bubbly and wallow in the feeling that, whatever is around the corner, you are prepared and have therefore, already improved your situation.

Thank you for reading this.

You have reached the end of the book. You are your own person and your life is out there waiting for you!

Your boss is a bastard and despite this you have started to focus your anger and frustration on generating positive outcomes for yourself. Congratulations on making such a healthy and *powerful* move.

Good for you!

Everyone is entitled to do work they enjoy, to work for reasonable people and to have a fulfilling life.

Let your boss rot.

Use your Personal Survival Kit to move yourself forwards.

You can do it!

Let's go...

Personal Survival Kit

Belonging to _____

Date compiled _____ / _____ / _____

Touchstones

Say these out loud either in the car on the way to work, or when looking in the mirror first thing in the morning.

I am not an antelope
I am smart
I have talents
I have a right to be me
My talents have not evaporated over night
I am learning
I will be fulfilled
I can change my life
I am prepared for the future

To download a copy of your Personal Survival Kit, please visit: www.richardmaun.com

1. Diamond Days of Fulfilment (Page 40)

Think about the days when I excelled.
What did I do?
How did I feel?

2. Harvest my Strengths (Page 46)

What strengths are contained within my Diamond Days?
What skills, aptitudes, abilities do I feel I have?

I am really good at ...

3. My Support Group (Page 57)

Write down the names, e-mail addresses and mobile telephone numbers of four people who are my core support group. What can they do to help me?

1.

2.

3.

4.

4. Keeping my Ego in Sight (Page 81)

A My ego would like me to take the following baggage, which I can really do without.

List

B In order to make some progress I am prepared to do things differently. These include:

List

5. Threat and Hunger Inputs (Page 111)

A Threat inputs make him feel unsafe. I need to avoid doing the following things to him

List

B Hunger inputs are about an absence of something. I need to start doing the following things to avoid trouble.

List

6. The Serengeti Boss Type Model (Page 118)

Circle one:

The Serengeti Boss Type Model (SBTM)

Crocodile
Snap

Lion
Roar

Stable

Meerkat
Eek

Elephant
Trumpet

Unstable

Non-Confrontational   **Confrontational**

7. Field Research (Page 140)

When my boss is angry, or upset, or really stressed his behaviour gets more extreme. He tends to say, or do the following:

8. Travelling Light (Page 152)

A The things I will take with me if I need to leave the business are:

List

_____

_____

_____

_____

_____

_____

_____

_____

B The money I am owed includes:

Item	£

9. Dealing with my Boss (Page 160)

Positive, healthy behaviour to deal more effectively with my boss includes:

10. Grounding Techniques (Page 164)

I will practise the following things to help me remain calm when faced with a wild animal and a dangerous situation.

1.

2.

3.

4.

11. Tomorrow is a Fresh Start (Page 176)

A My preferred options are:

B One thing I am going to do to make a start on them is:

12. My Desired Outcomes (Page 186)

I will work towards the following happy outcomes in order to increase my inner health:

Fulfilling Job Tasks
Tomorrow
Next Month
After 6 Months
After 2 Years

Training and Development
Tomorrow
Next Month
After 6 Months
After 2 Years

Home Life and Leisure Activities
Tomorrow
Next Month
After 6 Months
After 2 Years

Salary
Tomorrow
Next Month
After 6 Months
After 2 Years

13. My Dream Outcome (Page 187)

I can dream. My dreams are mine. I am entitled to a happy, healthy and fulfilling life.

And if I remain self-aware, make positive decisions, use my support group and take calculated risks, I will be in a stronger position to achieve my most fulfilling outcome, which is:

14. My First Step (Page 192)

A The first step I will take to head towards fulfilment is:

_____

_____

_____

_____

_____

_____

_____

B When I have completed this step my reward will be:

_____

_____

_____

_____

_____

_____

_____

_____

_____

_____

15. My CV (Page 192)

I have updated my CV and it is now:

Current

- Yes
- No

Smart

- Yes
- No

Accurate

- Yes
- No

Relevant

- Yes
- No

Superb

- Yes
- No

One billiant single page

- Yes
- No

16. Honesty Check (Page 192)

I have completed all parts of my Personal Survival Kit.

- Yes
- No

I have been really honest and not lied to myself.

- Yes
- No

I have decided to laugh and learn.

- Yes
- No

I have made a commitment to myself to have a fulfilling life.

- Yes
- No

I have a plastic bag available for emergency packing

- Yes
- No

17. Celebration (Page 192)

I am now prepared.

MY BOSS IS A BASTARD!
▦ Always
▦ Frequently
▦ Often
▦ Sometimes

However, I am not so scared and fed up because I am ready for the future. I have my Personal Survival Kit and I'm not afraid to use it. I can increase my fulfilment and inner health.

▦ Tick here upon completion of my Personal Survival Kit.

WELL DONE ME!

About the Author

Richard Maun is an international career turnaround specialist, lively conference speaker and engaging workshop facilitator. He combines Transactional Analysis in organisational settings with Lean thinking, practical operational experience and his own unique career management models. His executive coaching work has been described as 'powerful' and 'genuinely transformative' and his books have been translated across the world.

Richard now runs his own management development company, is a director of a training company and is a visiting lecturer to a leading UK university and in his work he uses Transactional Analysis and combines it with Lean thinking. He also works as a freelance business writer and has published four other books with Marshall Cavendish – *Bouncing Back, How To Keep Your Job, Job Hunting 3.0* and *Leave The B@$T@*DS Behind* – that look at how get going again after a career setback, how to excel in the workplace, how to get a job in a competitive world and how to set oneself up in business. All four are based on real-life experiences and contain practical tips and engaging stories.

Richard can be contacted via:
Modern Careers Blog: www.richardmaun.com
Facebook Page: Richard Maun – Modern Careers
LinkedIn: Richard Maun
Twitter: @RichardMaun
Skype: richardmaun
Business: www.primarypeople.co.uk